LINESCAPES

CREATIVE PATTERNS
FOR COLORING

BY MIRELI

I0476966

AUTHOR'S NOTE

I think the most important thing you can do if you want to tap into your creative space and release stress is to engage in mindfulness activities. Every creative flash has a different process, but quietness and stillness are key ingredients. If you have tried meditation, and find it difficult to sit still or clear your thoughts, I encourage you to try coloring and painting. Our patterned landscapes are an invitation to lose yourself in the fun process of coloring. It may inspire you, or at least keep you entertained for hours.

LINESCAPES came about by my daughter's insistence. She persuaded me to start the collection after seeing my geometrical patterns of mountains and meadows. They have been favorite subjects of my drawings. I find ideas in all sorts of places, road trips in New England, parks, and travels in South America.

While working on LINESCAPES, I learned a few interesting facts about patterns. Pattern recognition is taught at a very early age. Our brains are wired to recognize patterns, and this innate ability is becoming increasingly understood in science. By coloring patterned landscapes, you can now connect internally by engaging in a mindfulness activity while indulging in a mentally pleasurable experience.

Learn...
        Create...
                Inspire...

Mireli

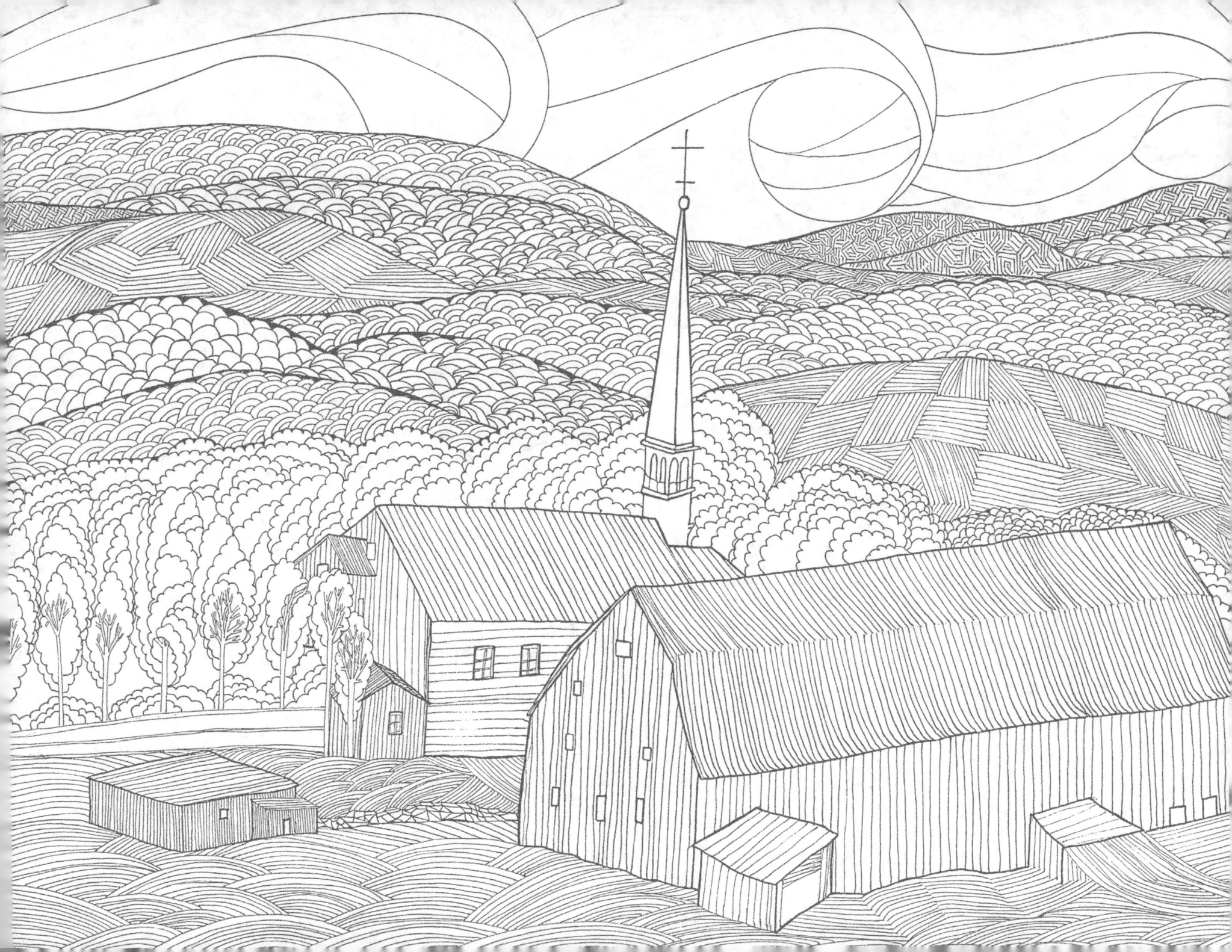

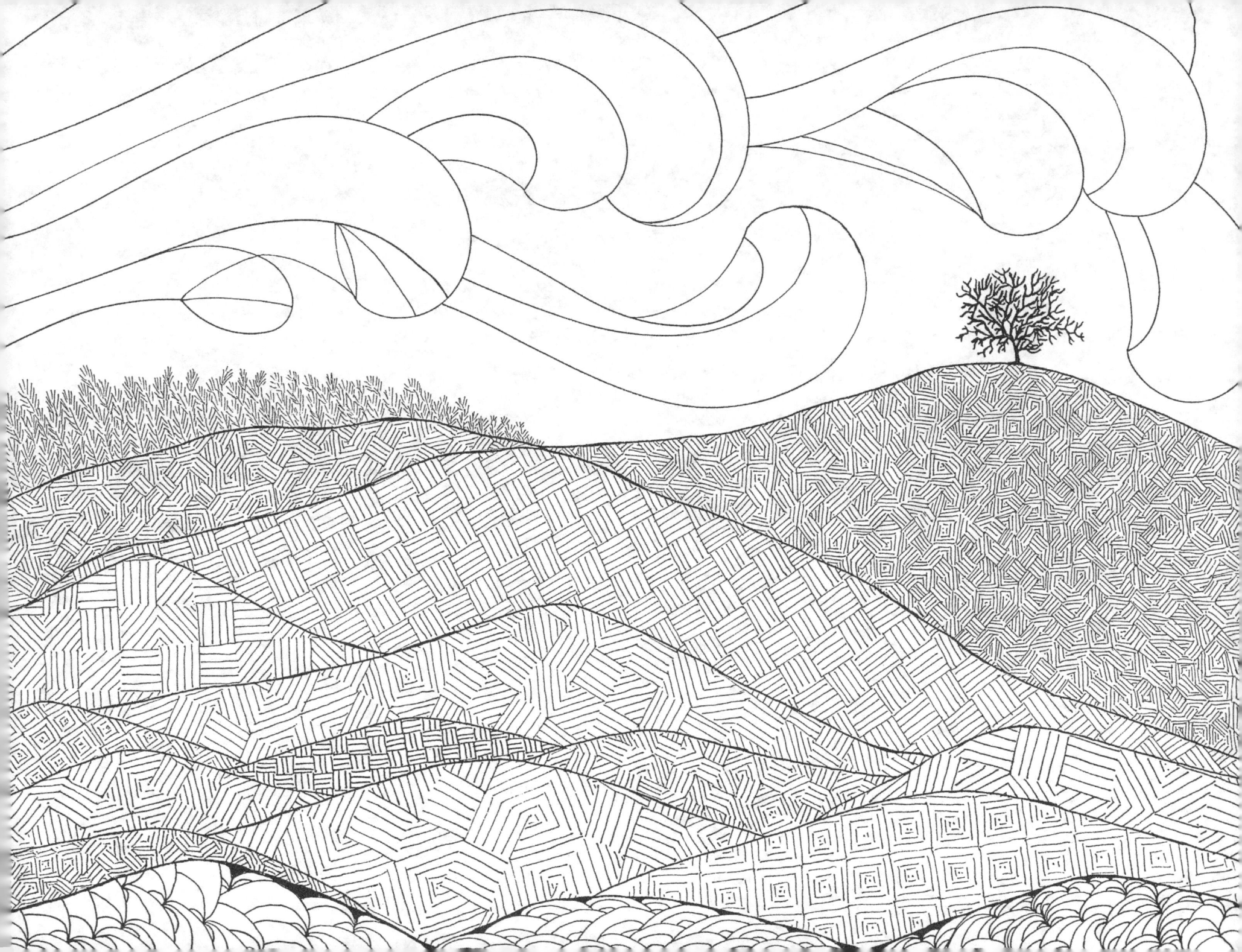

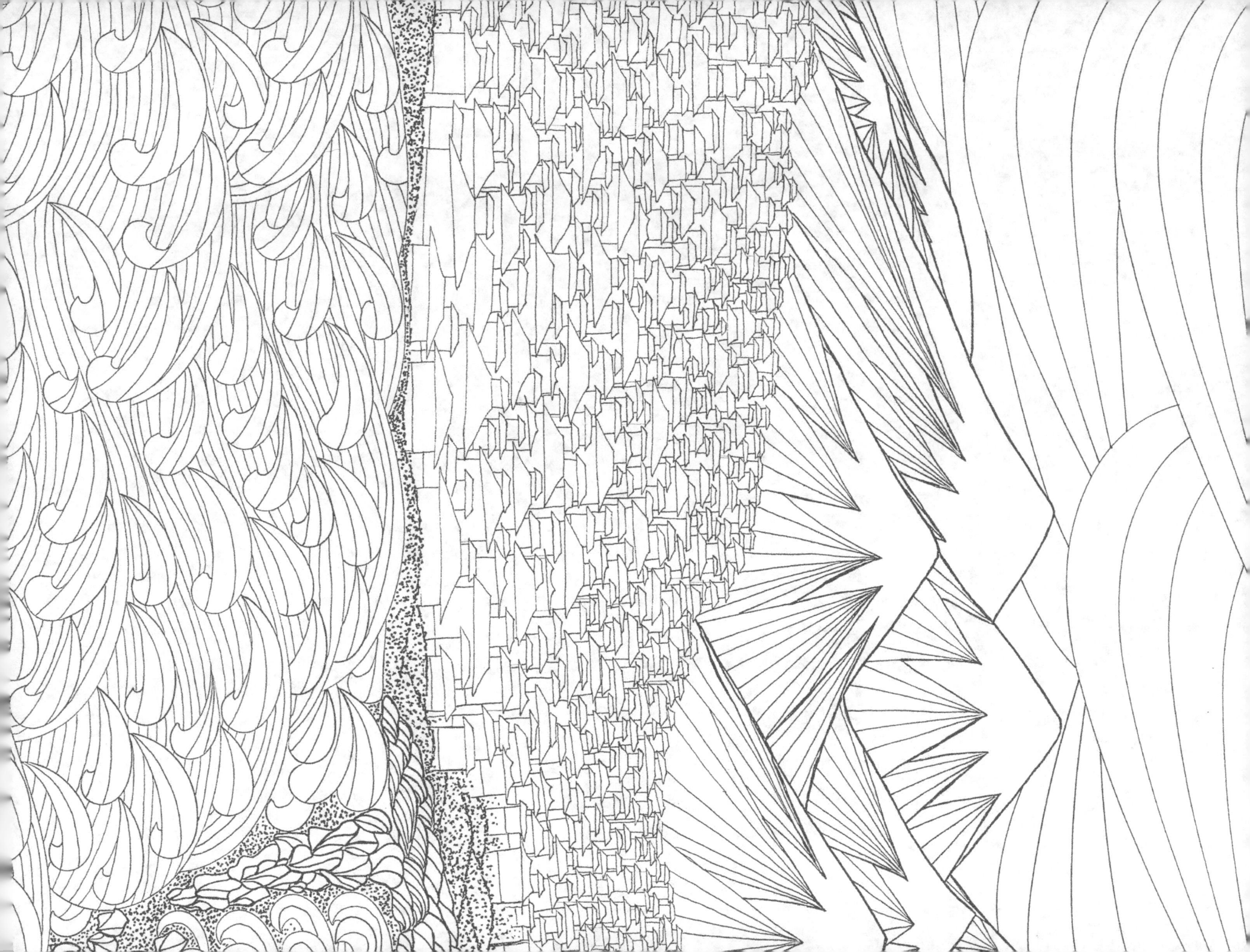

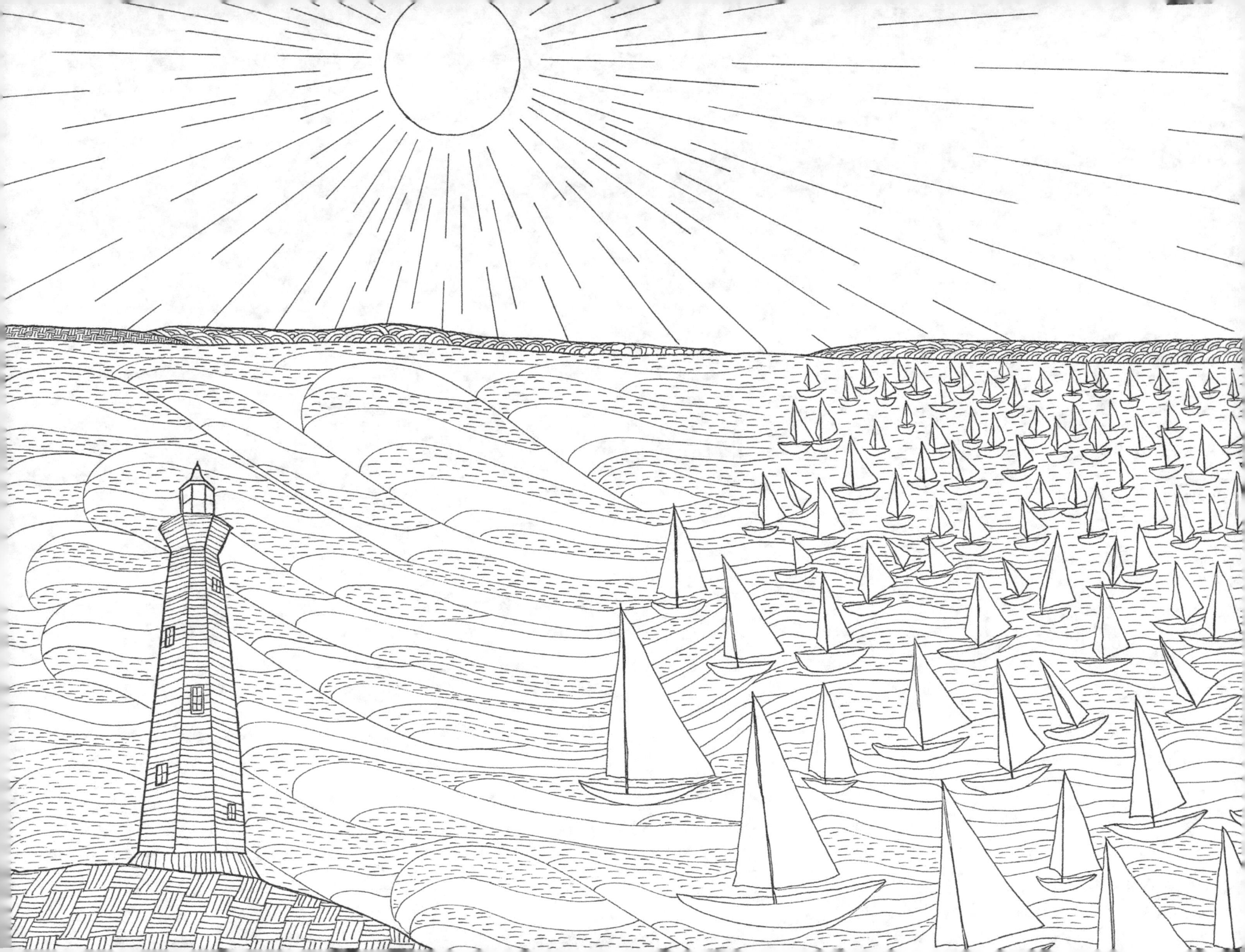

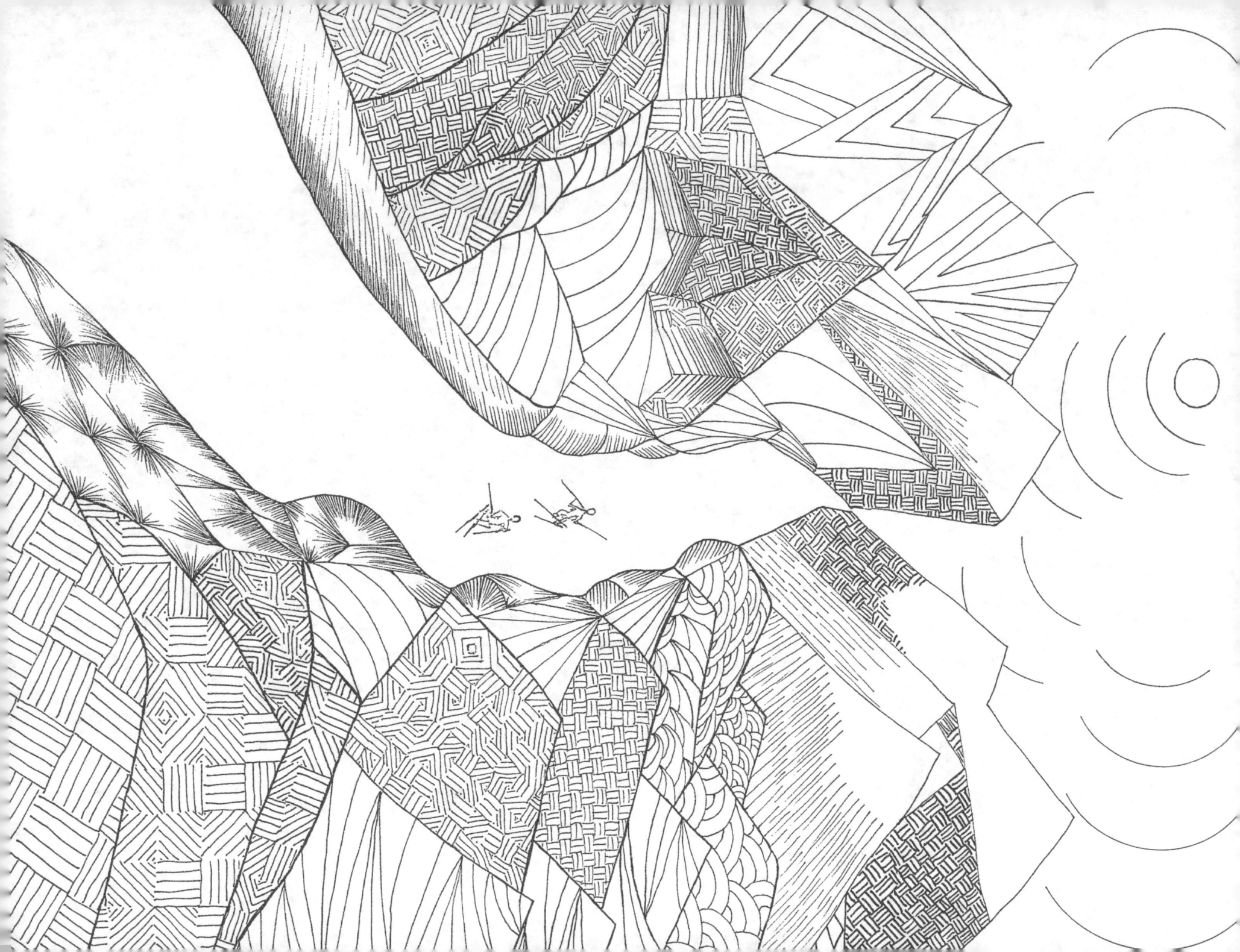

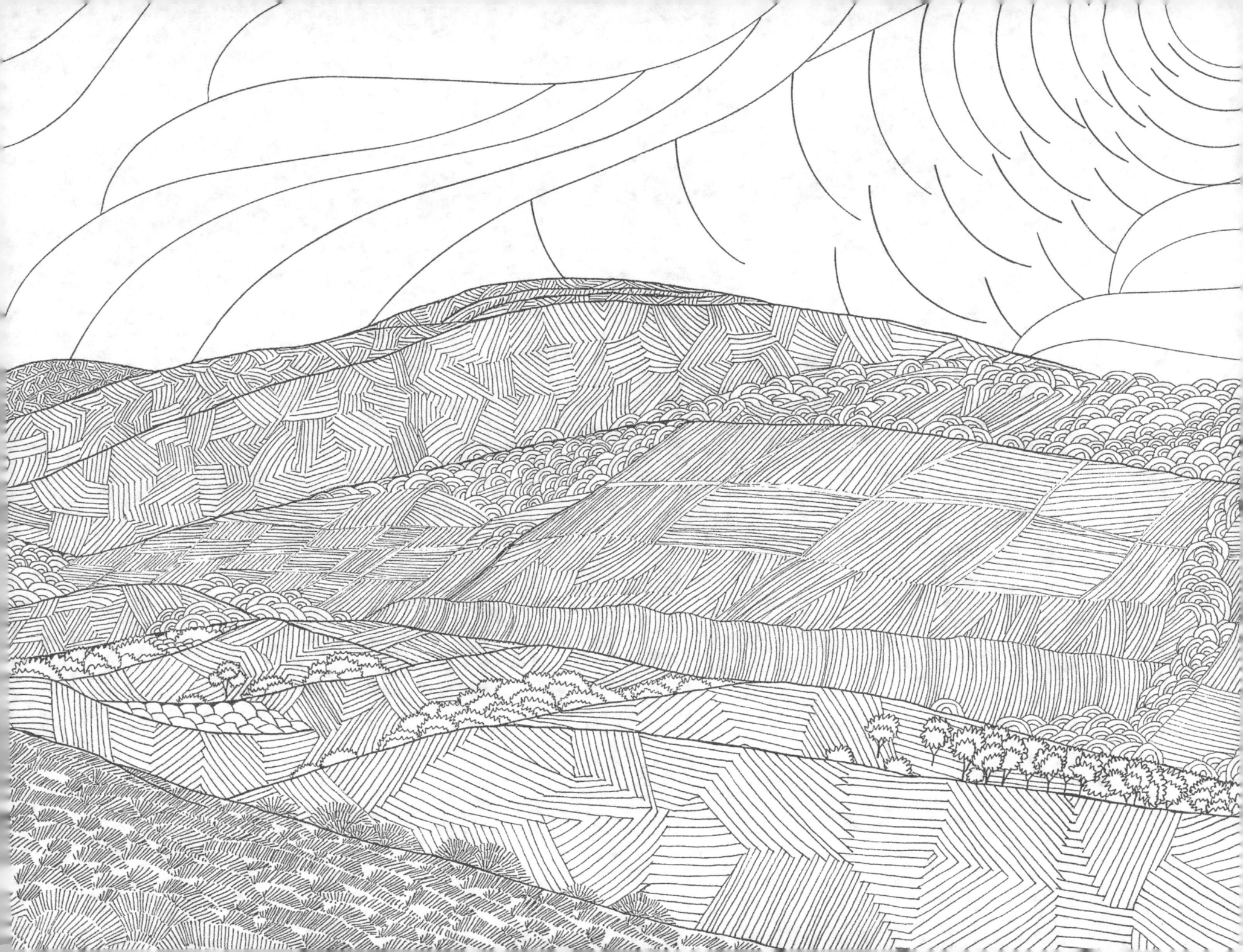

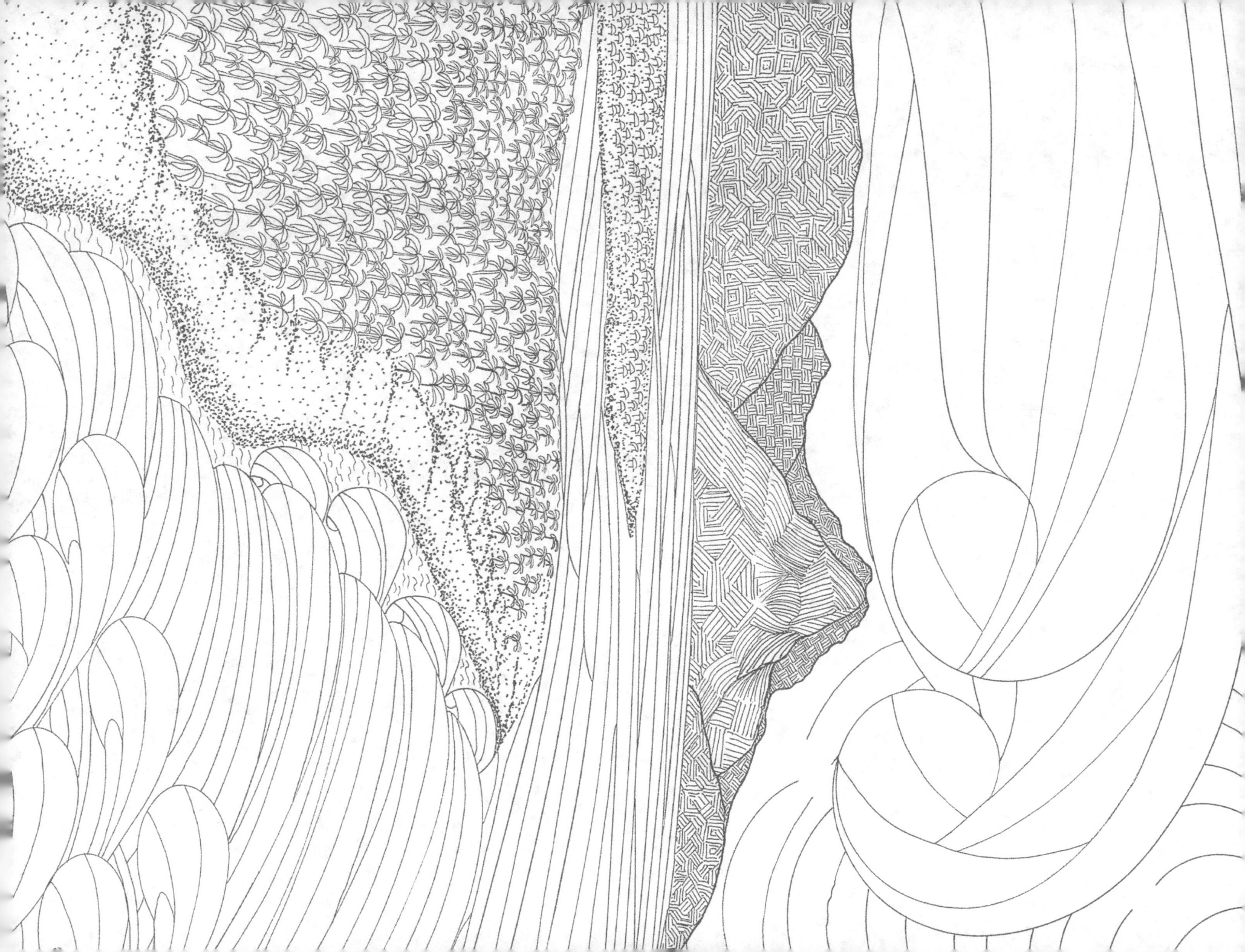

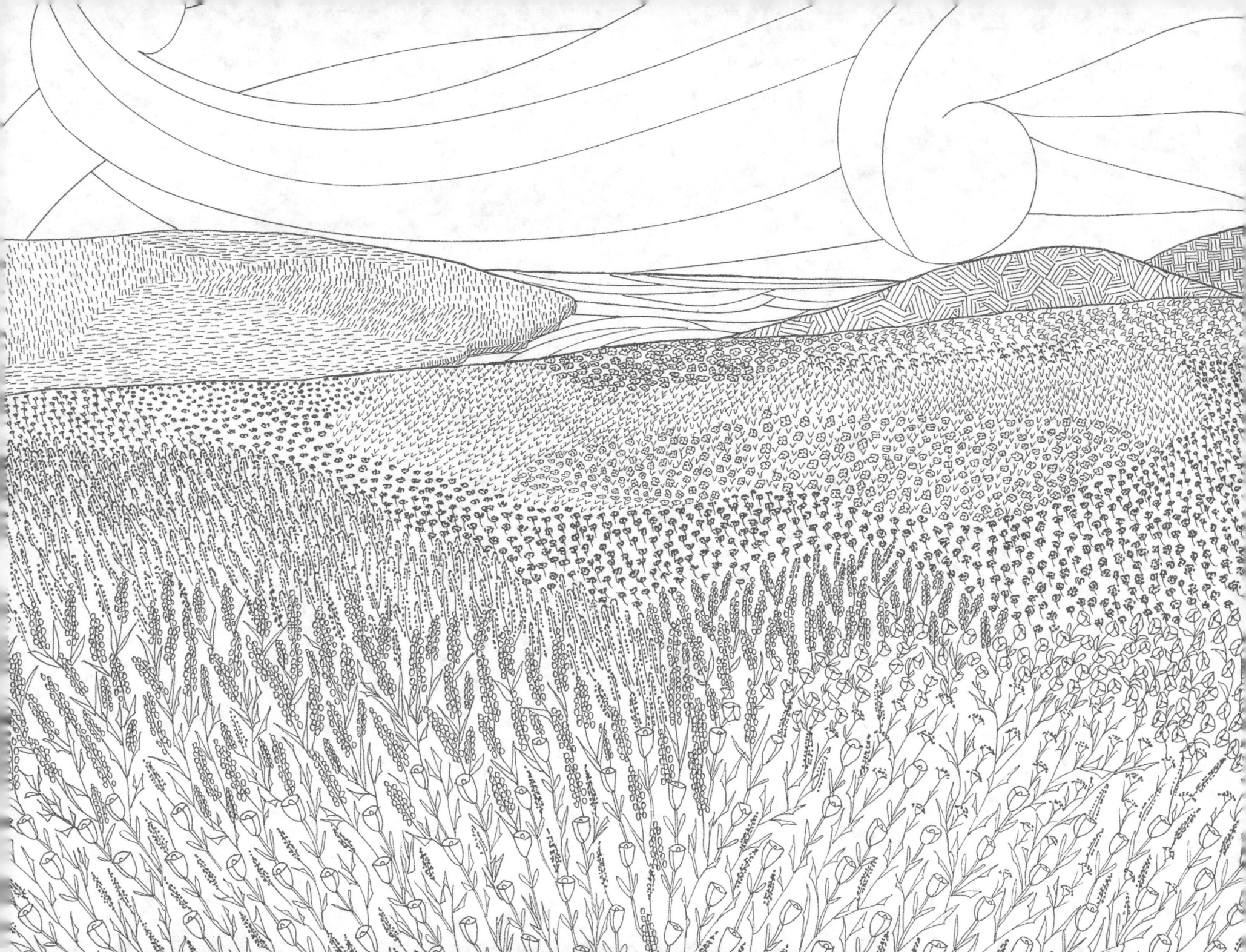

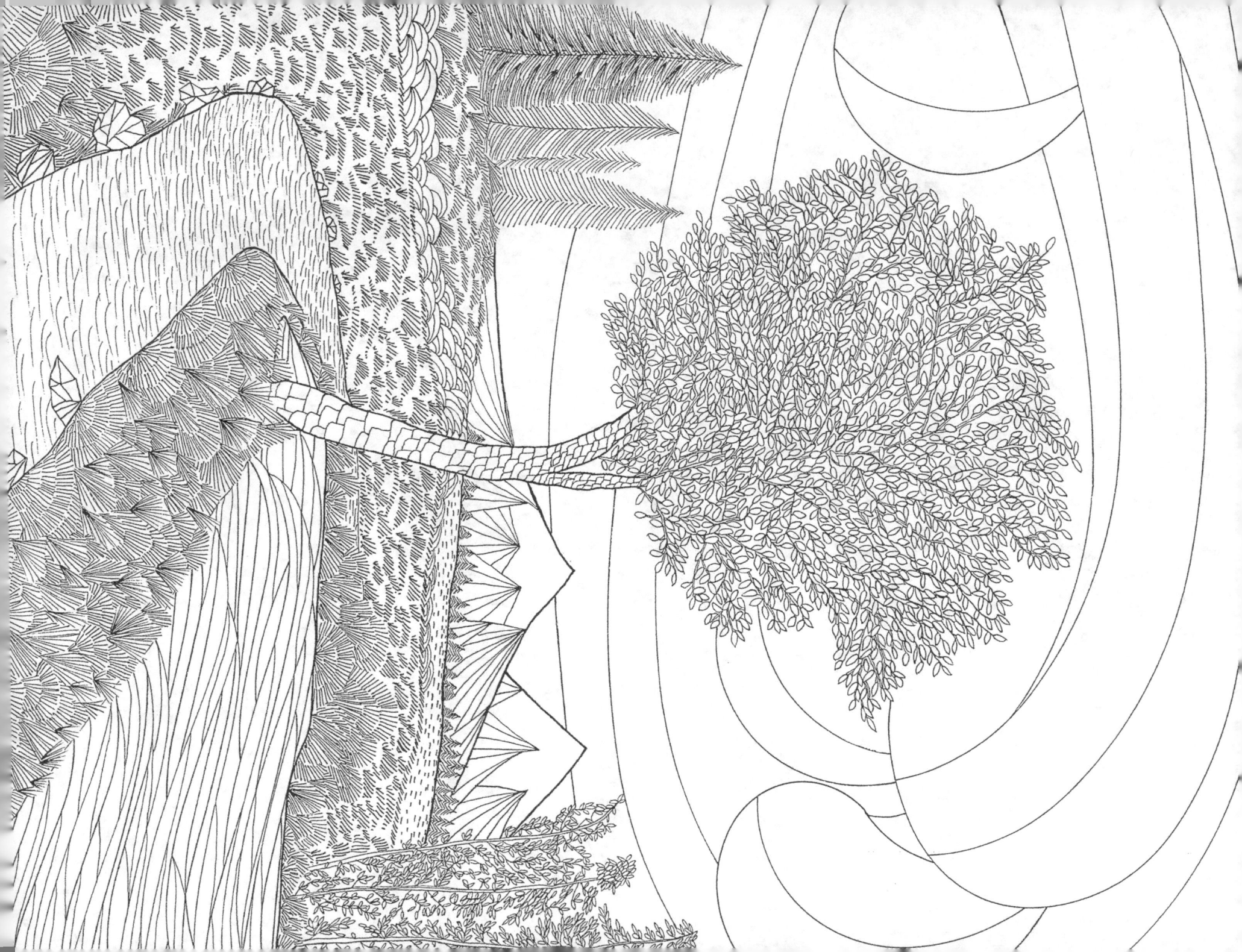

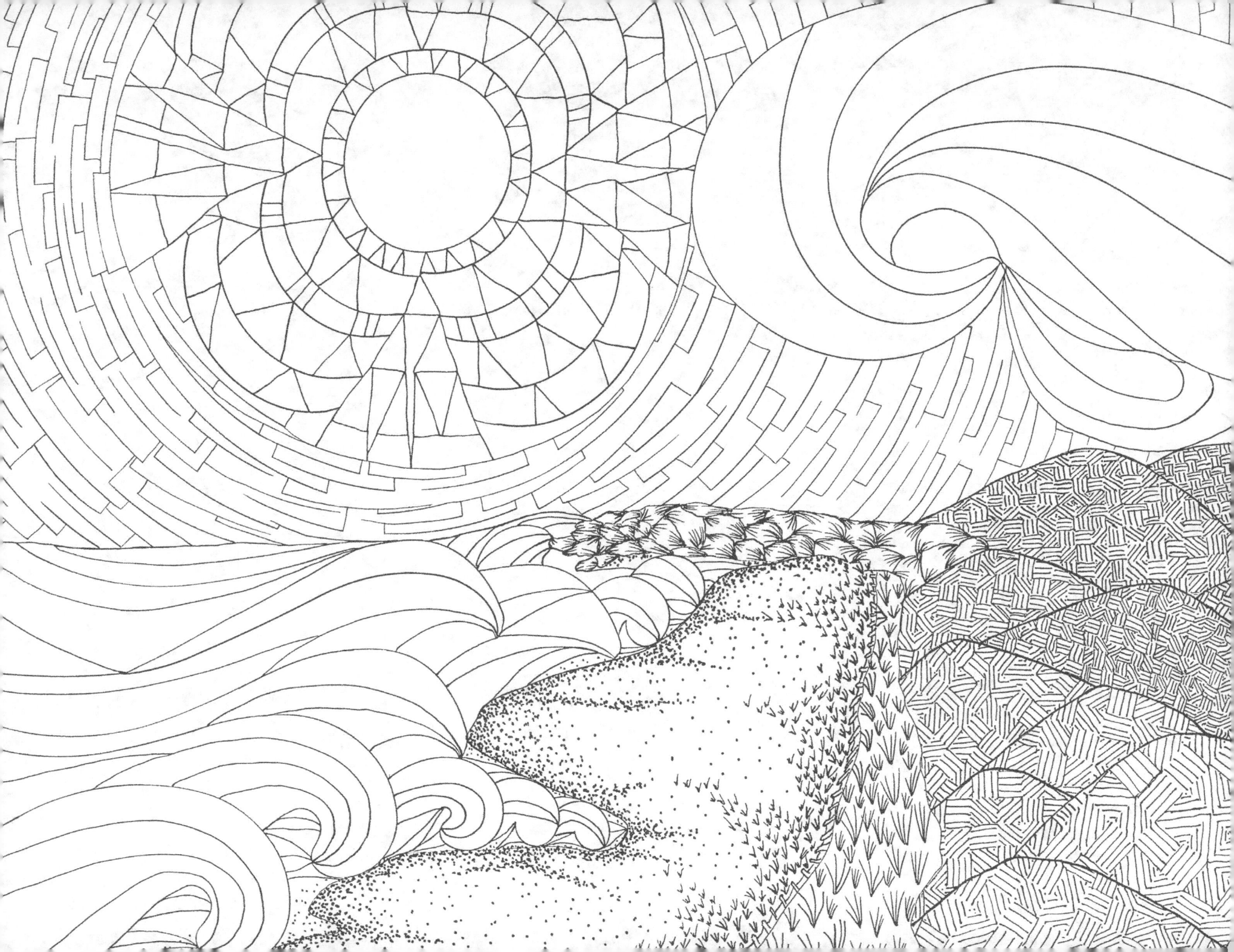

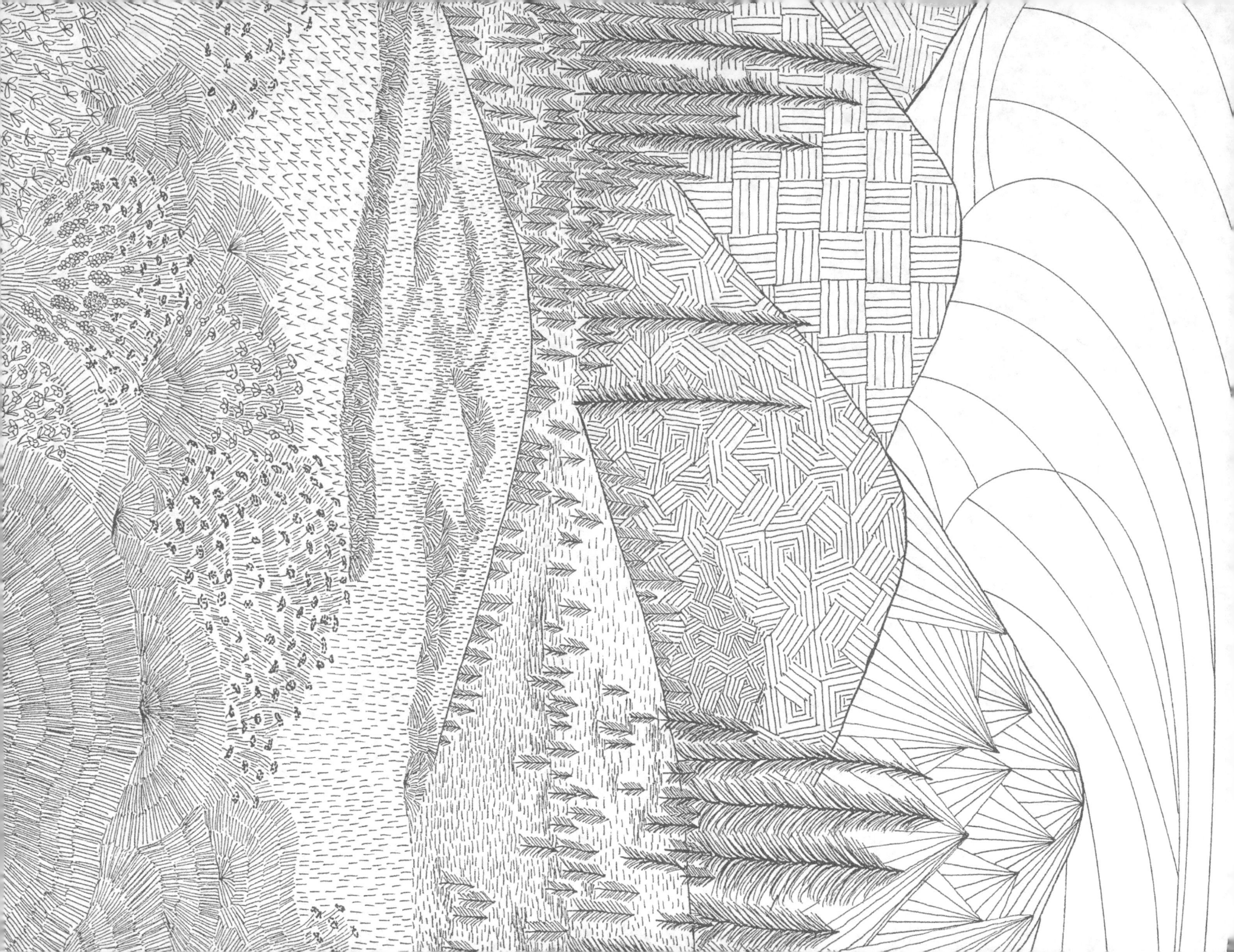

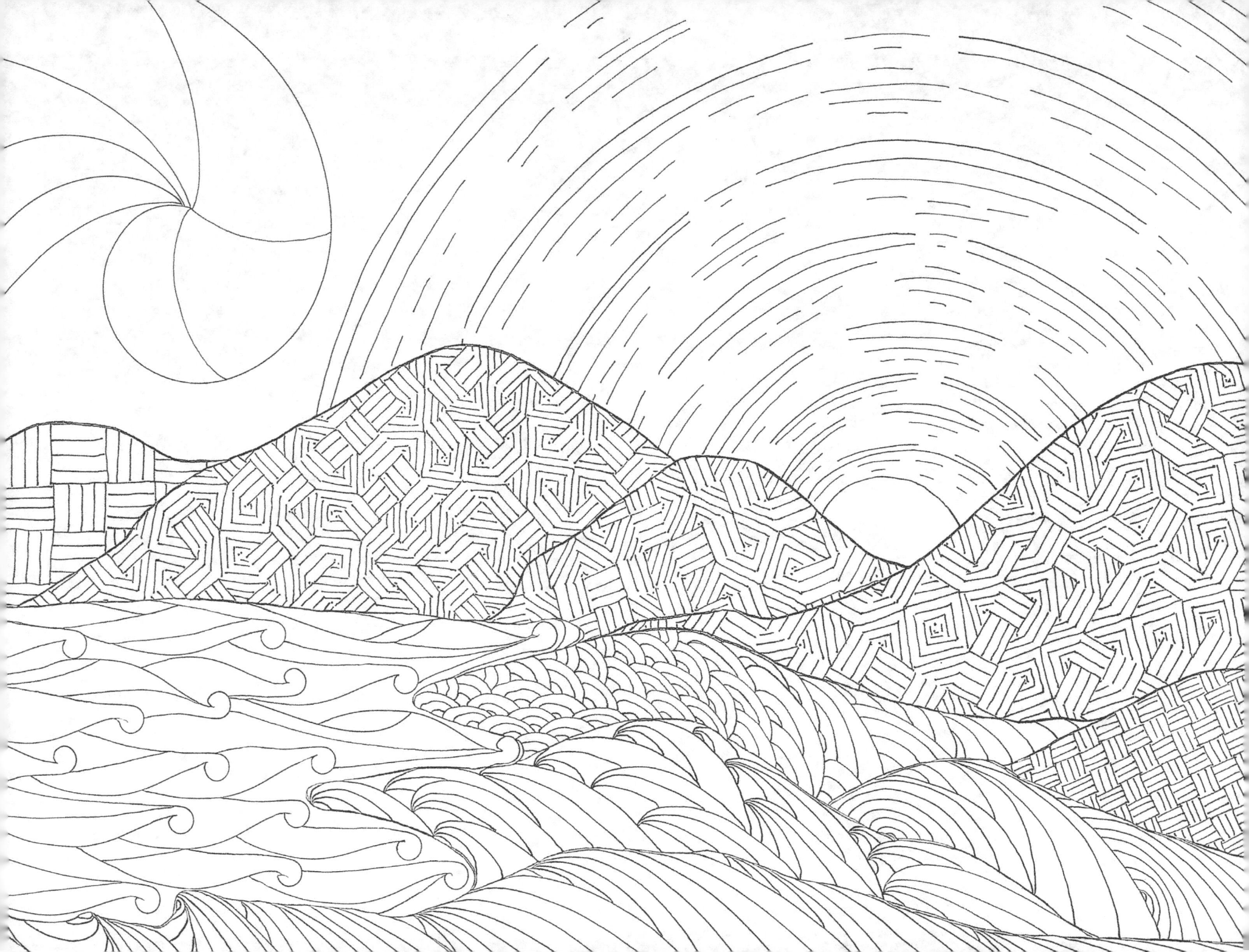

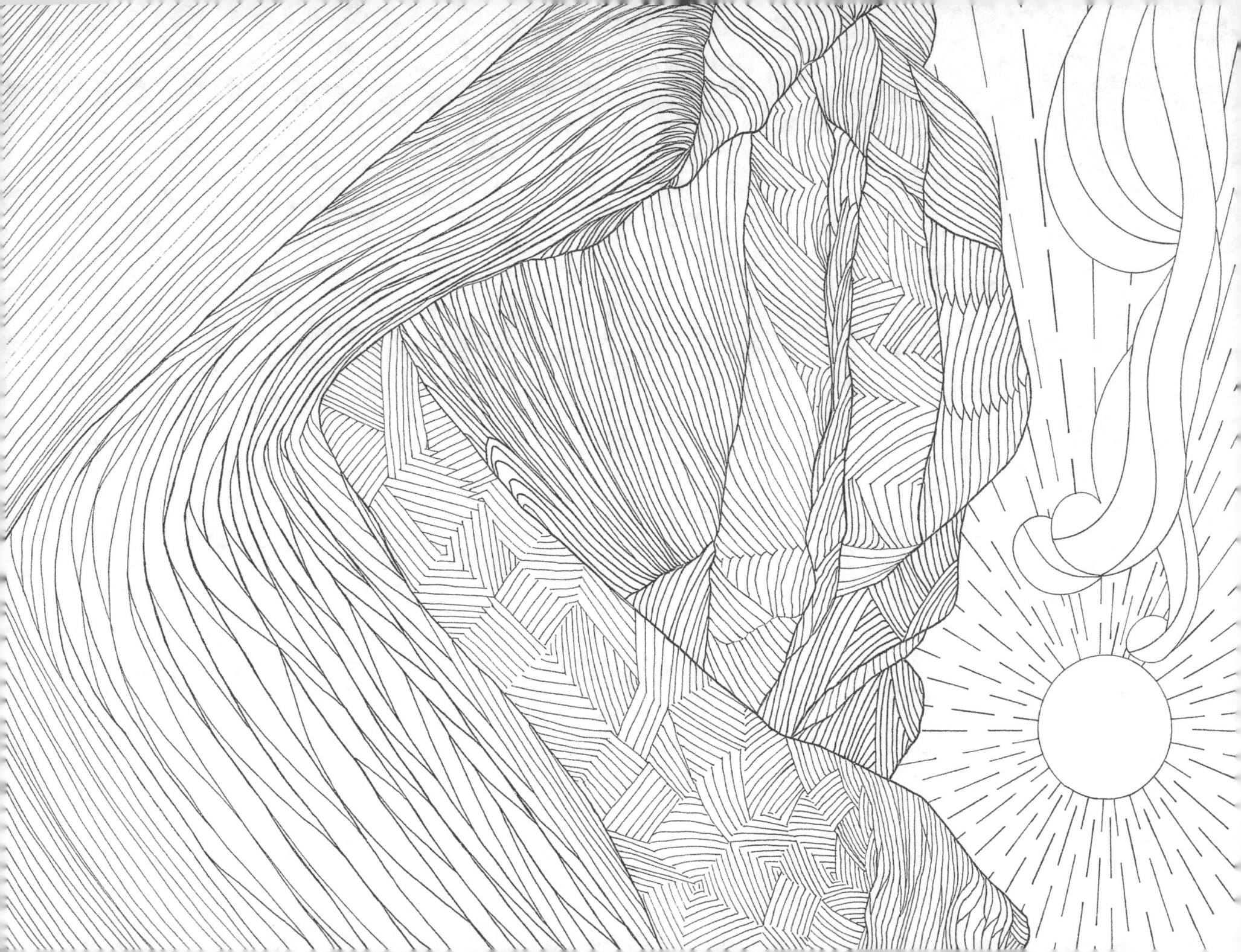

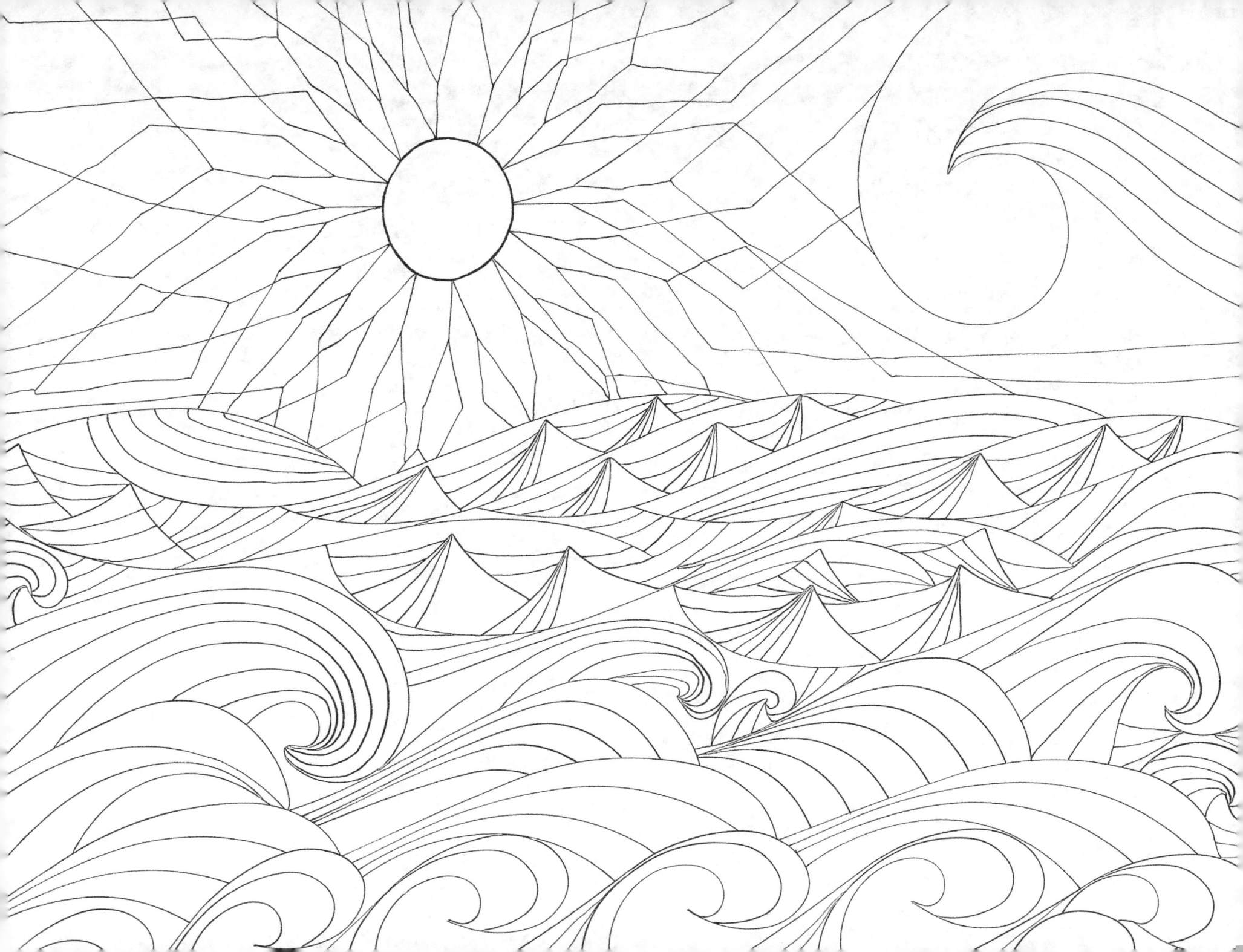

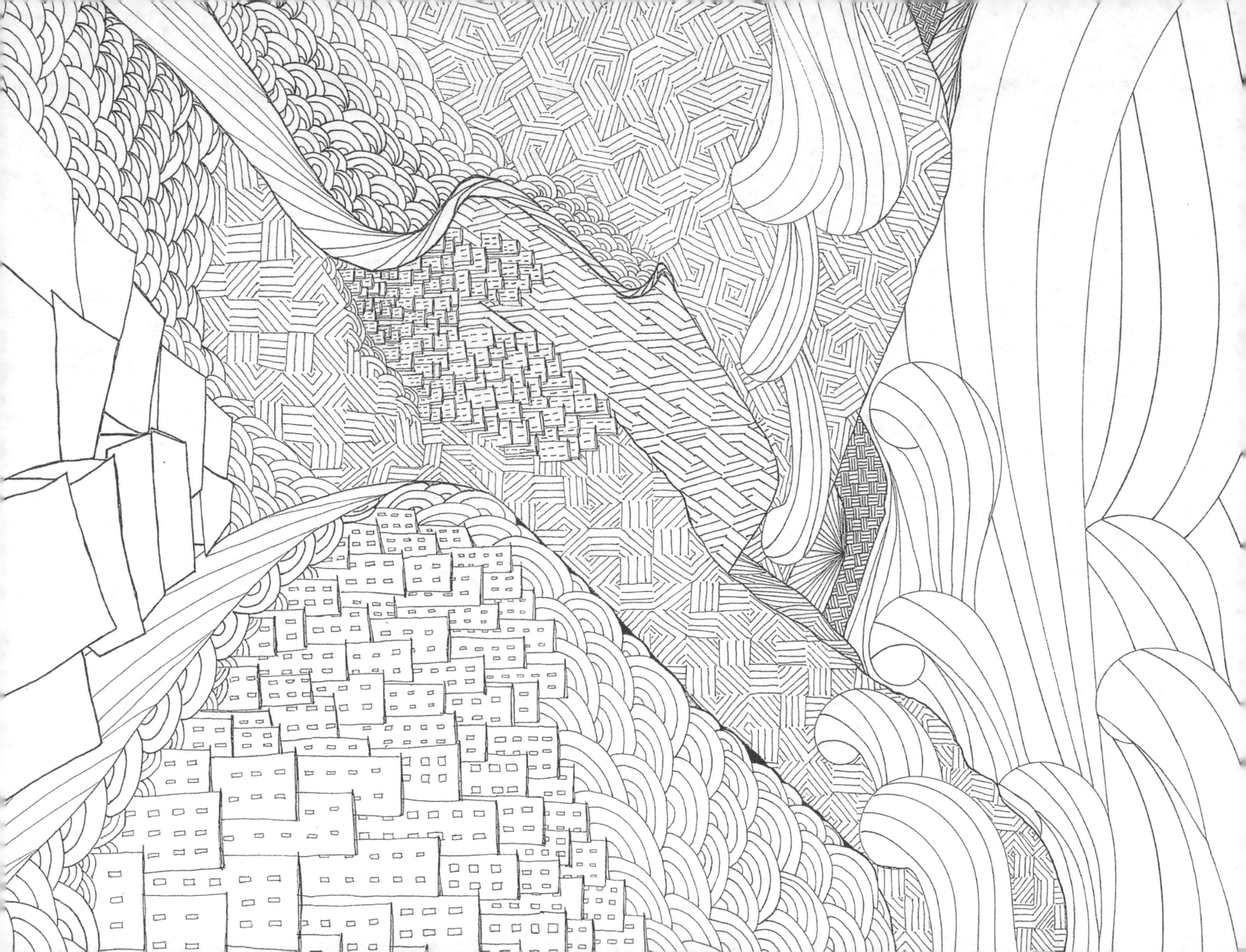

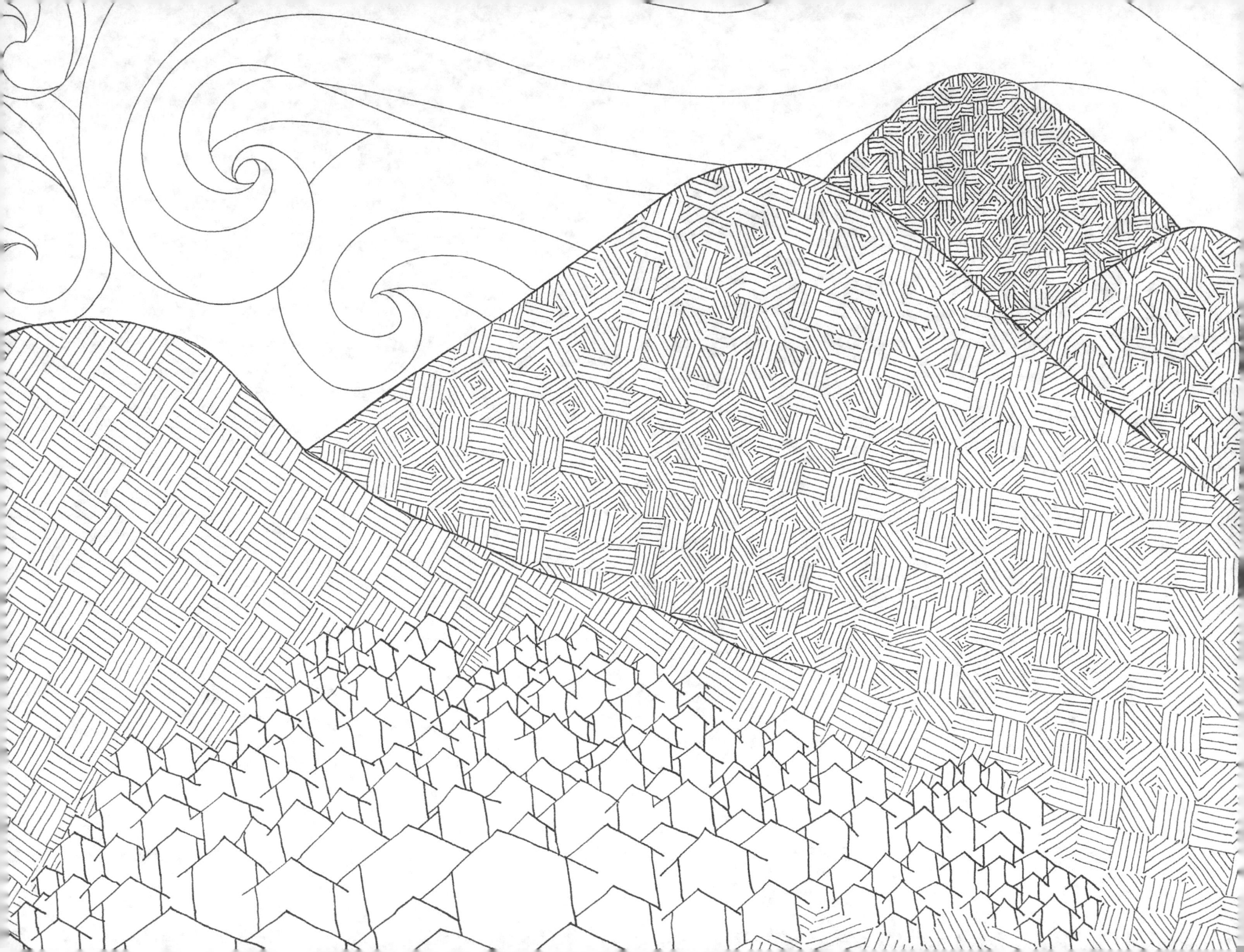

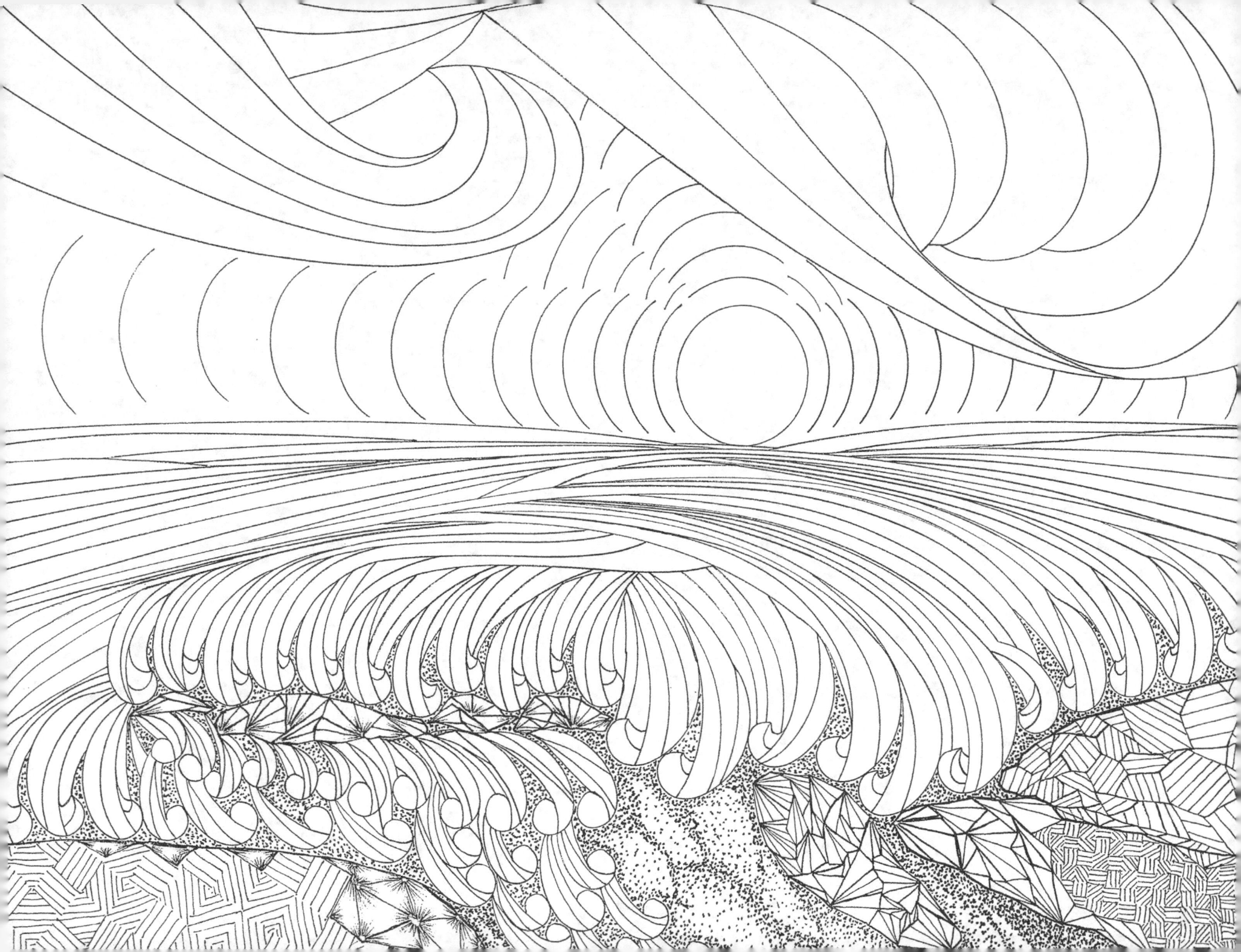

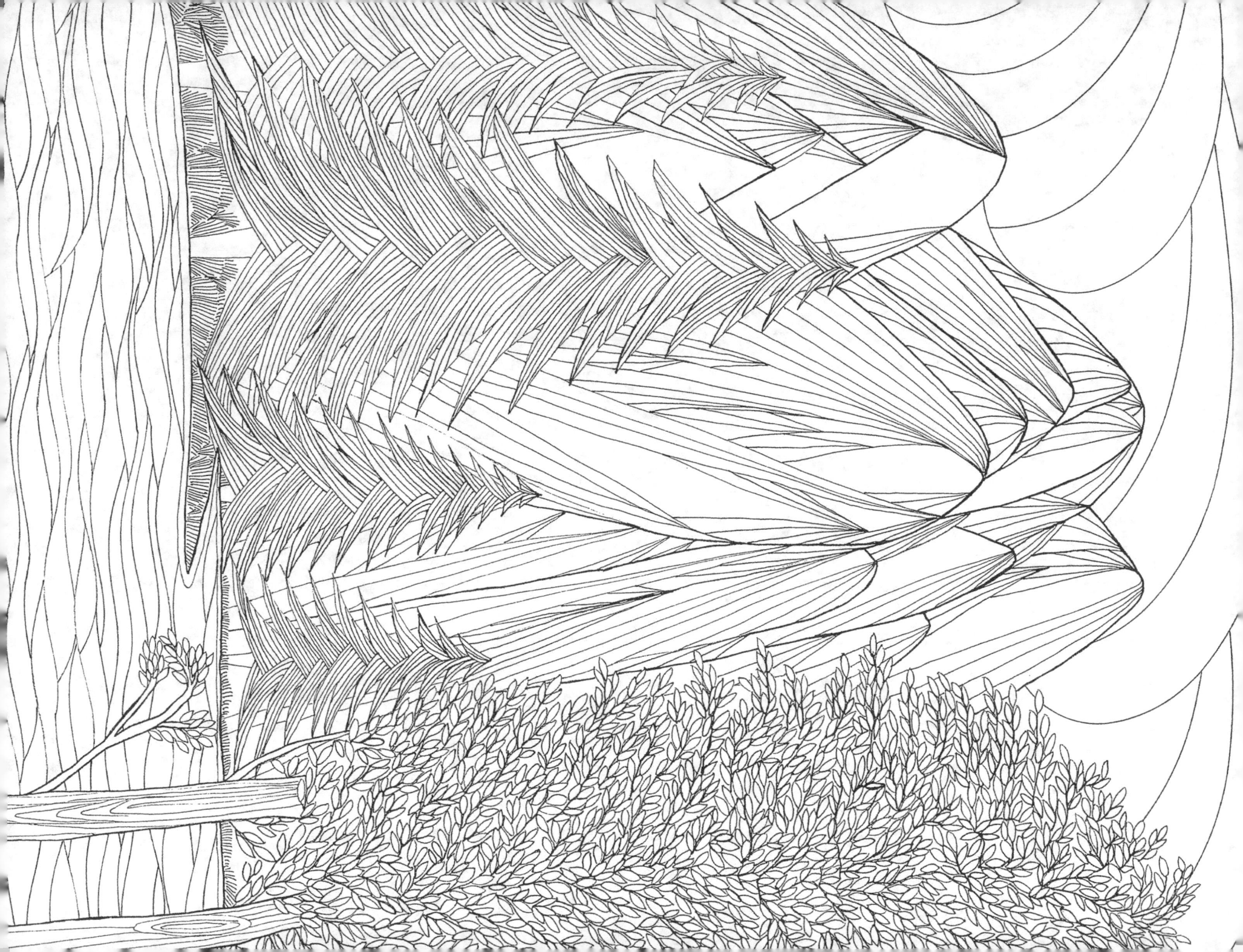

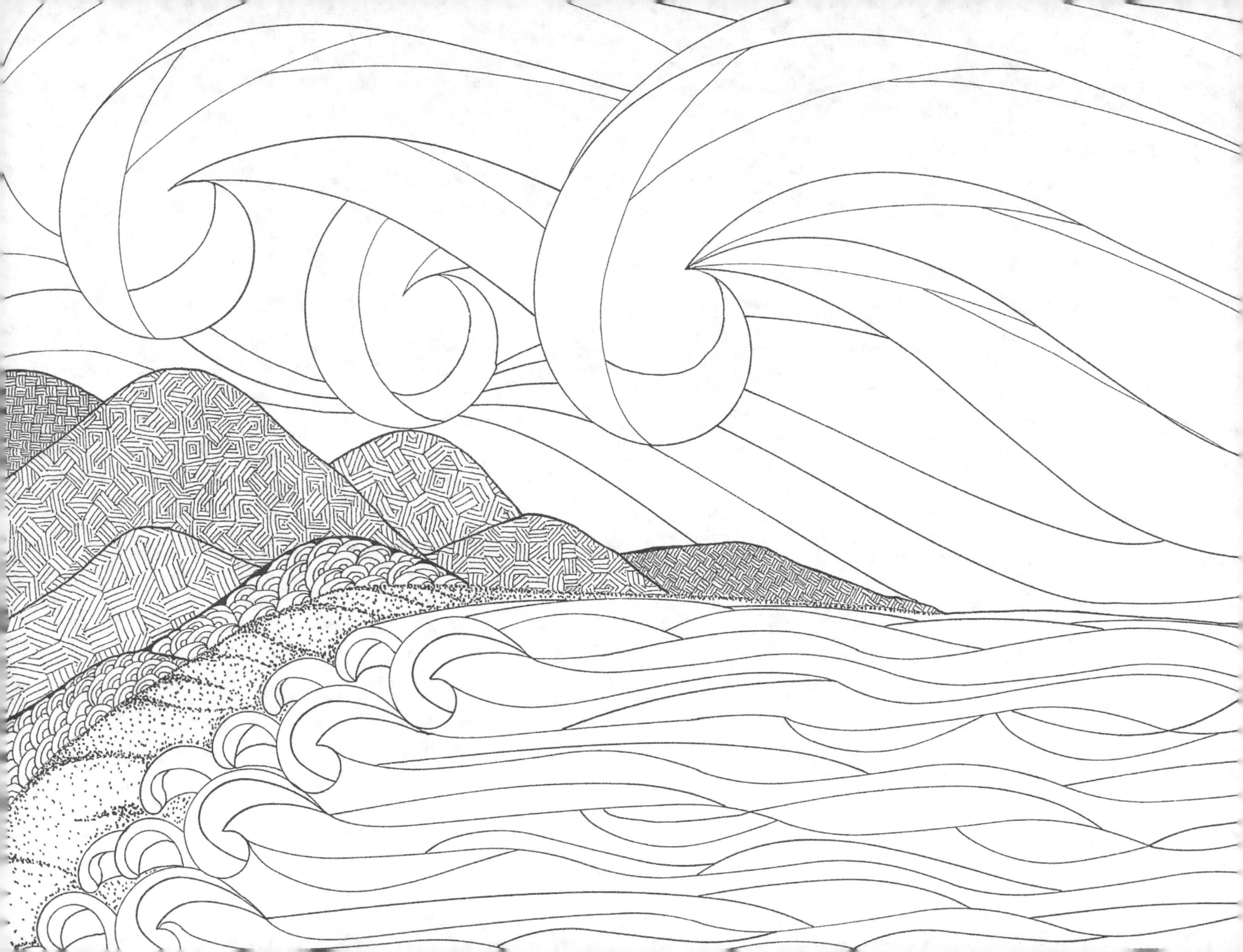

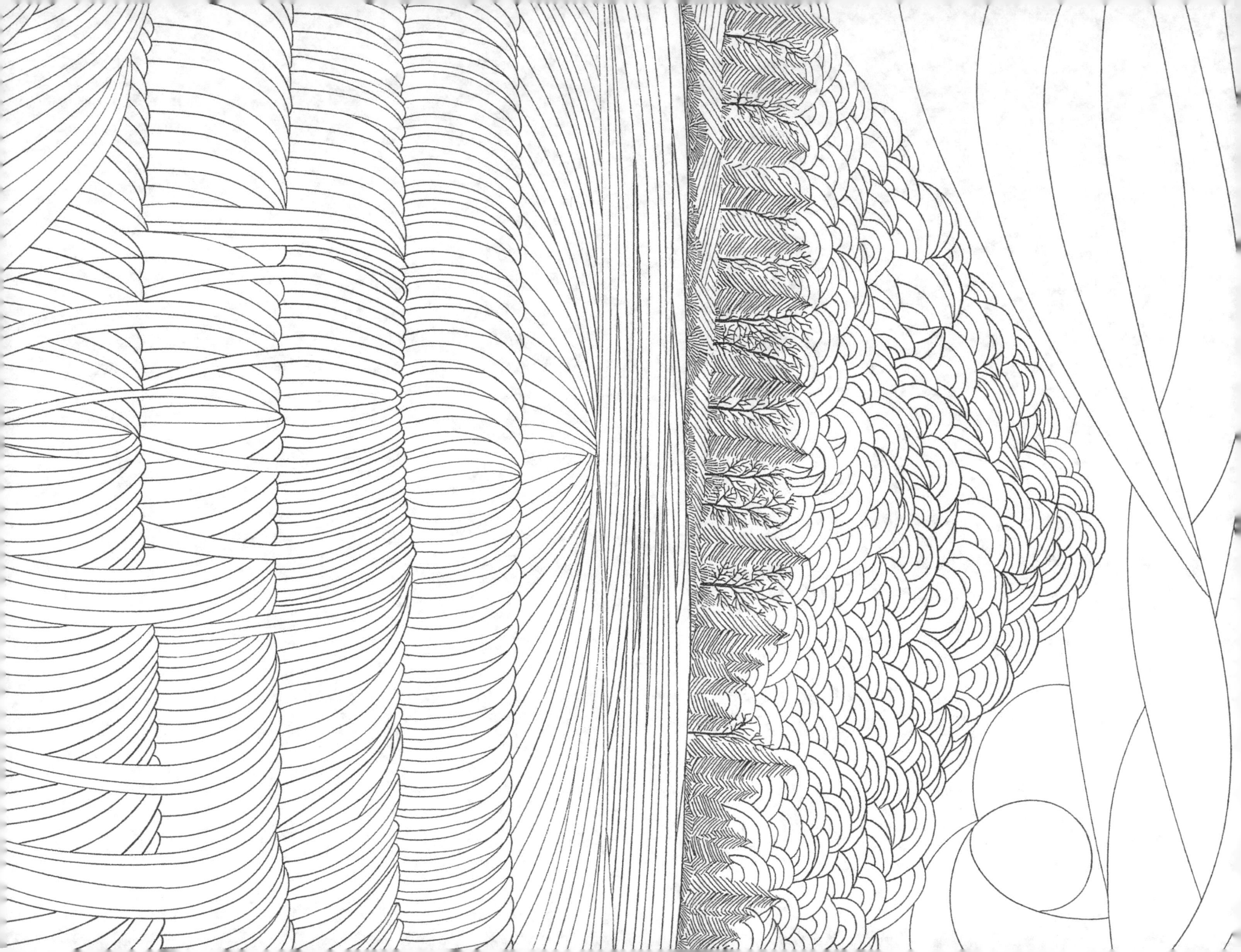

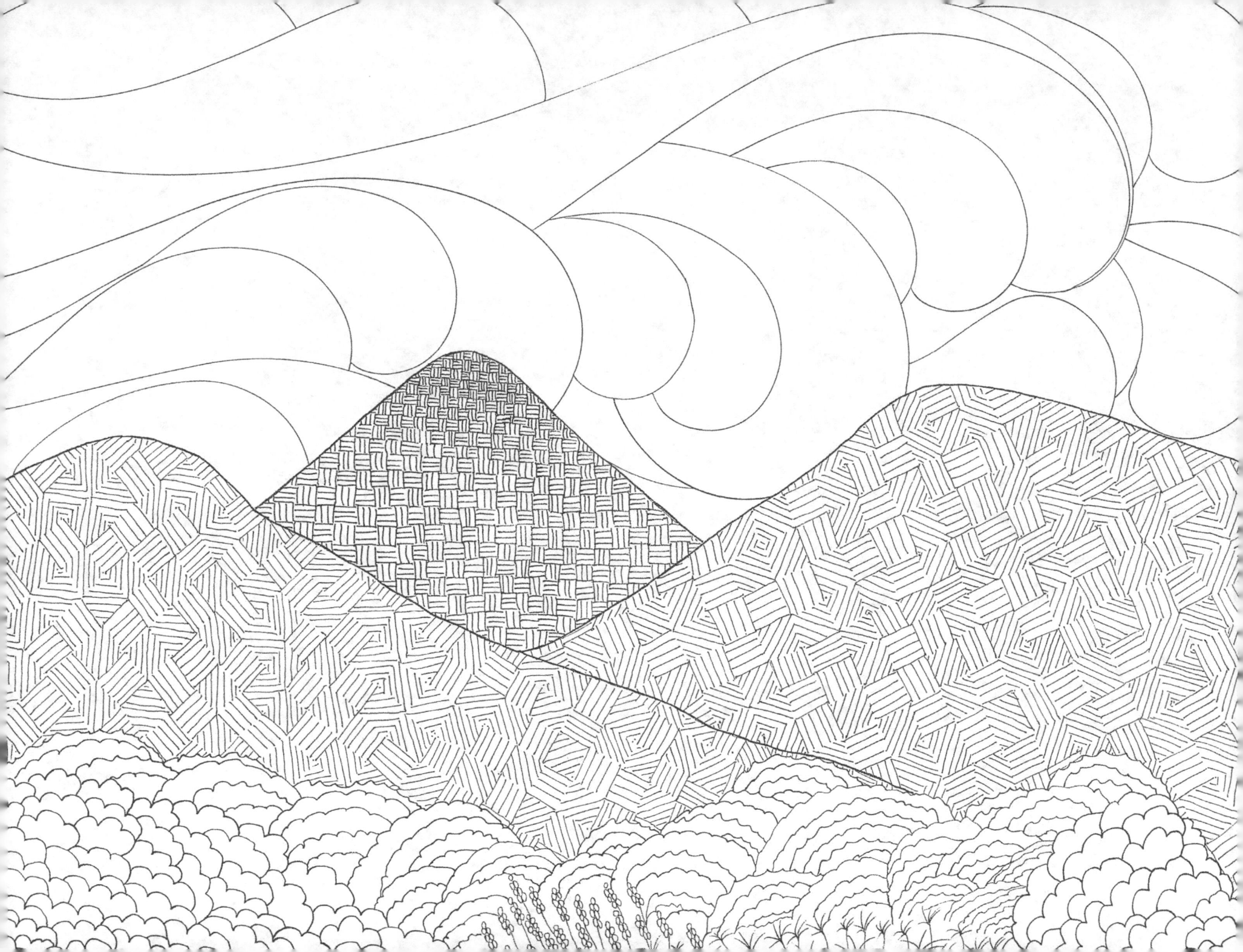

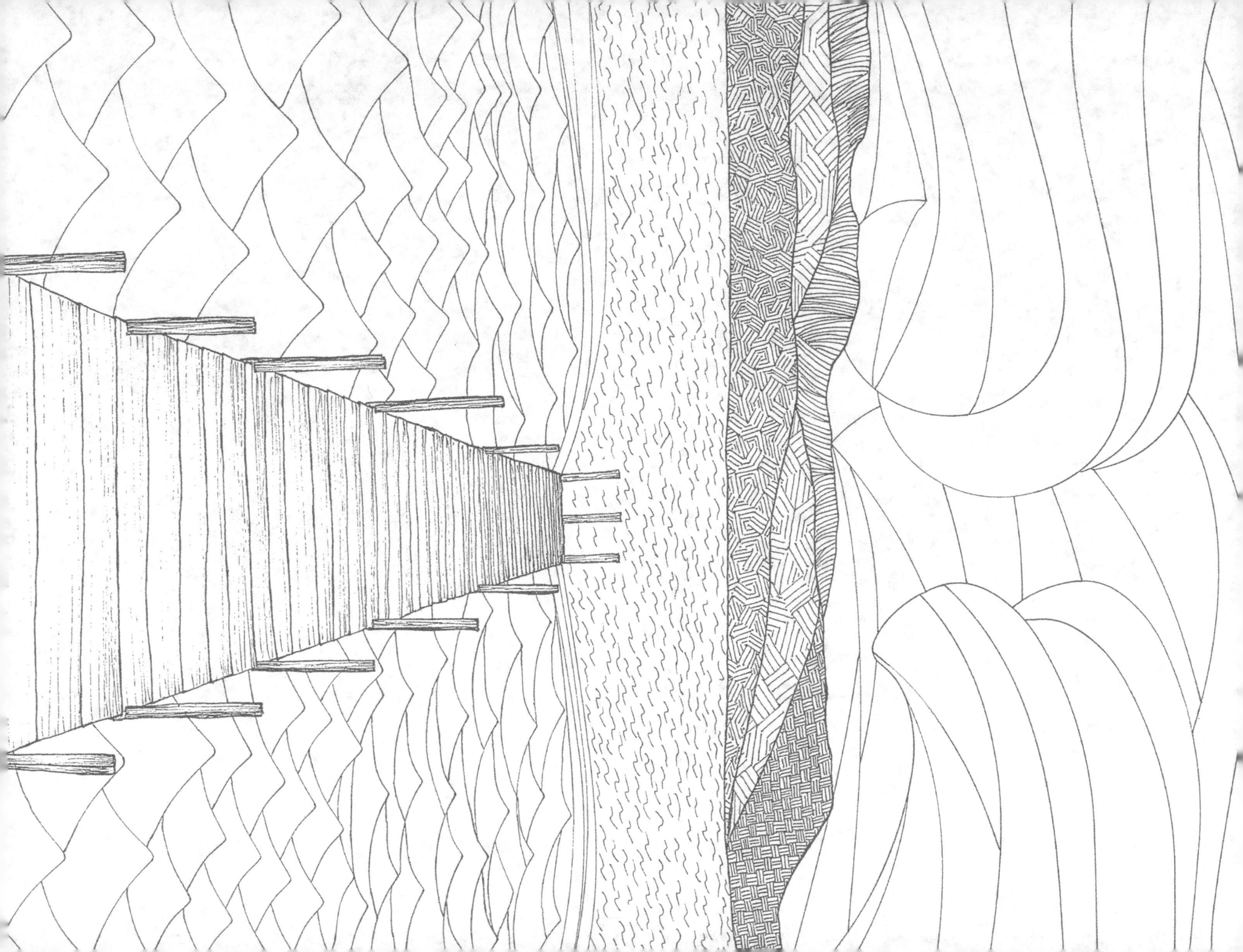

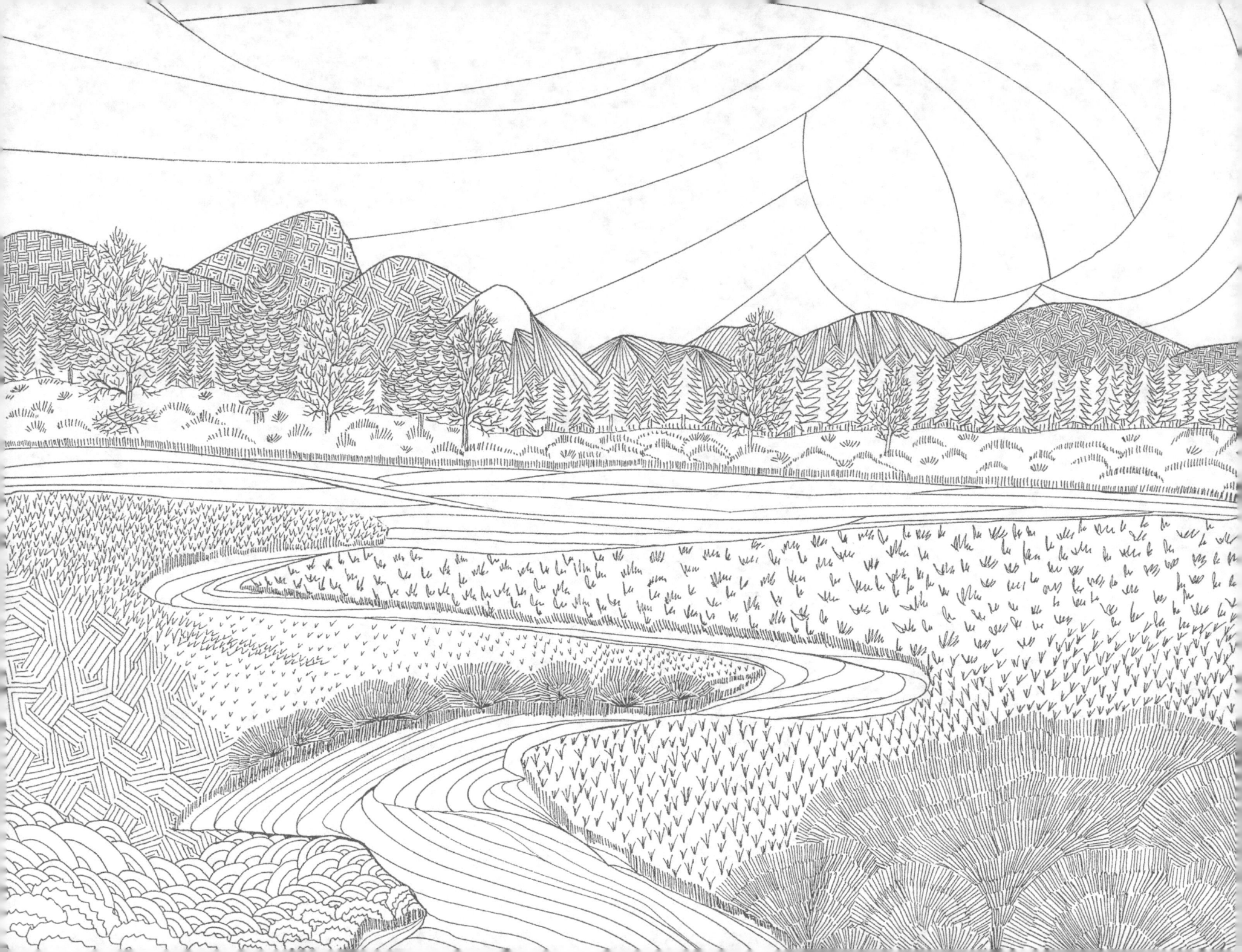

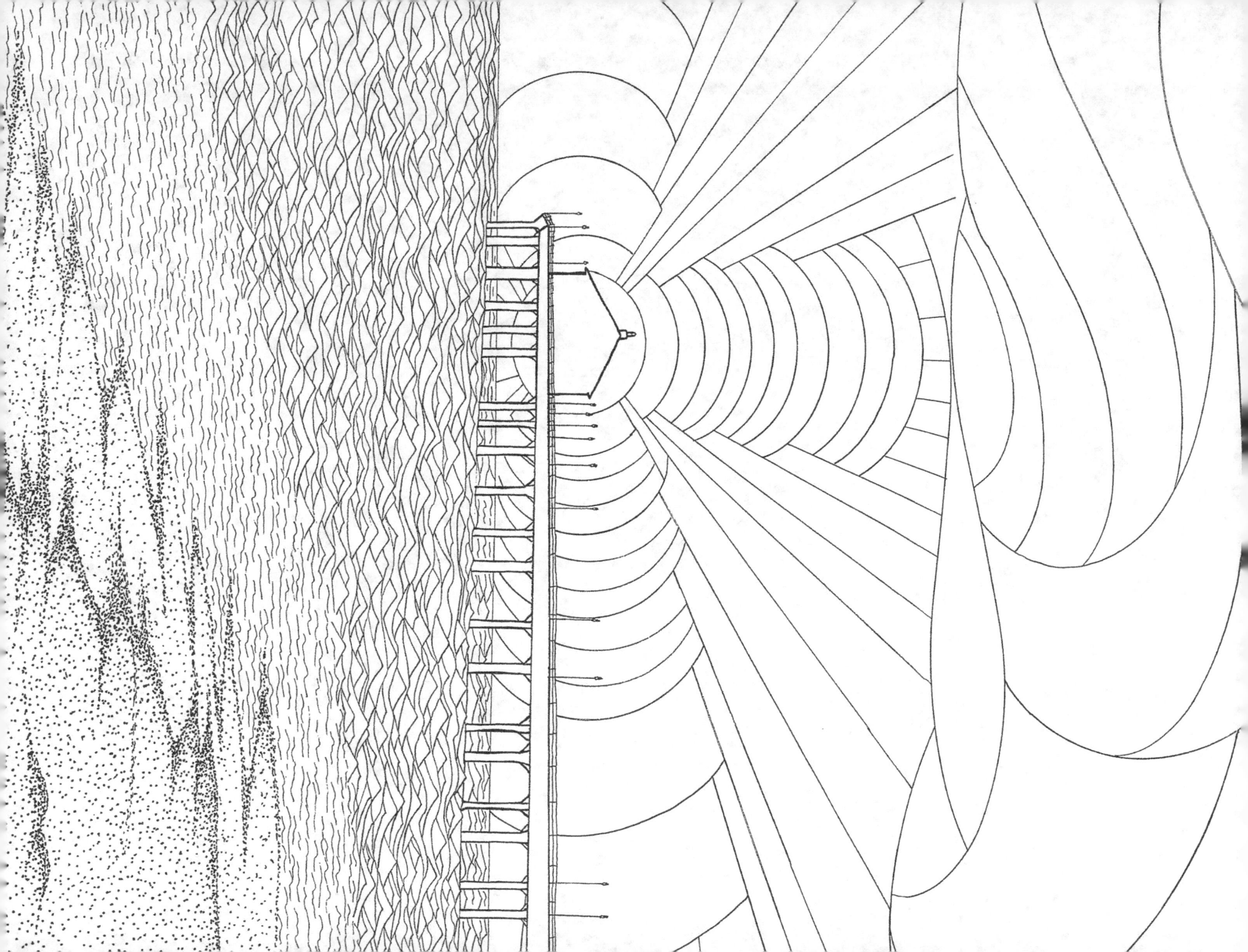

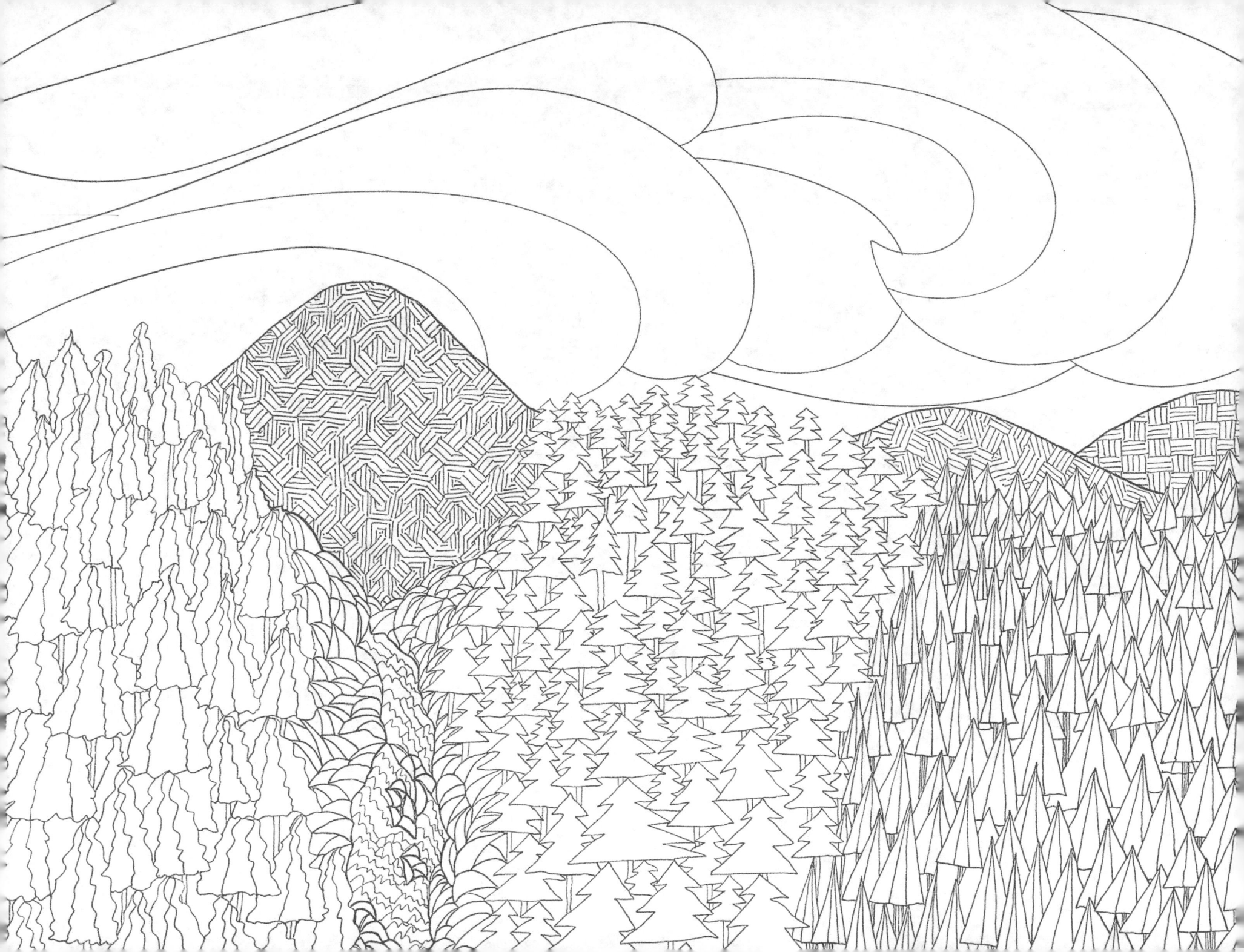

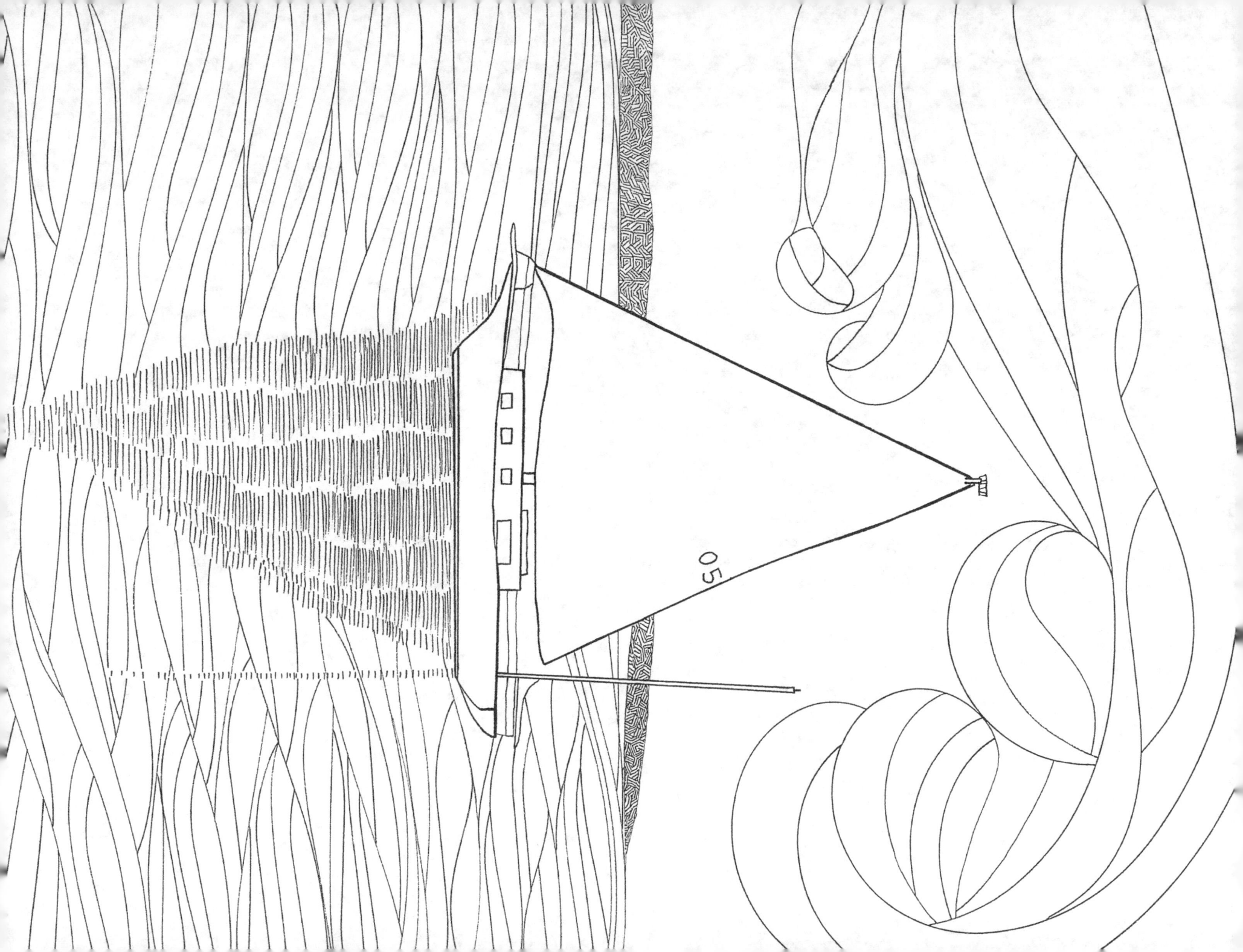

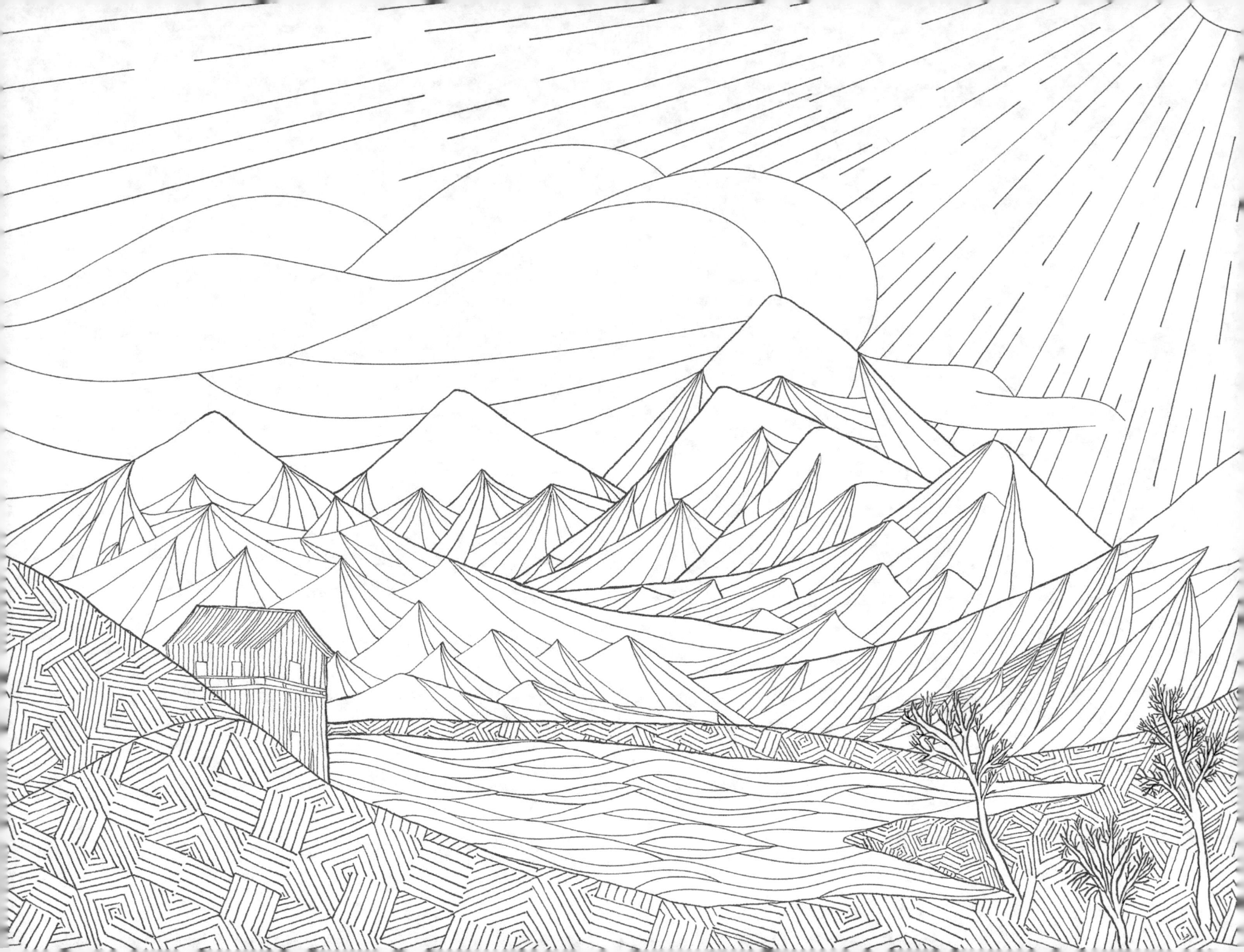

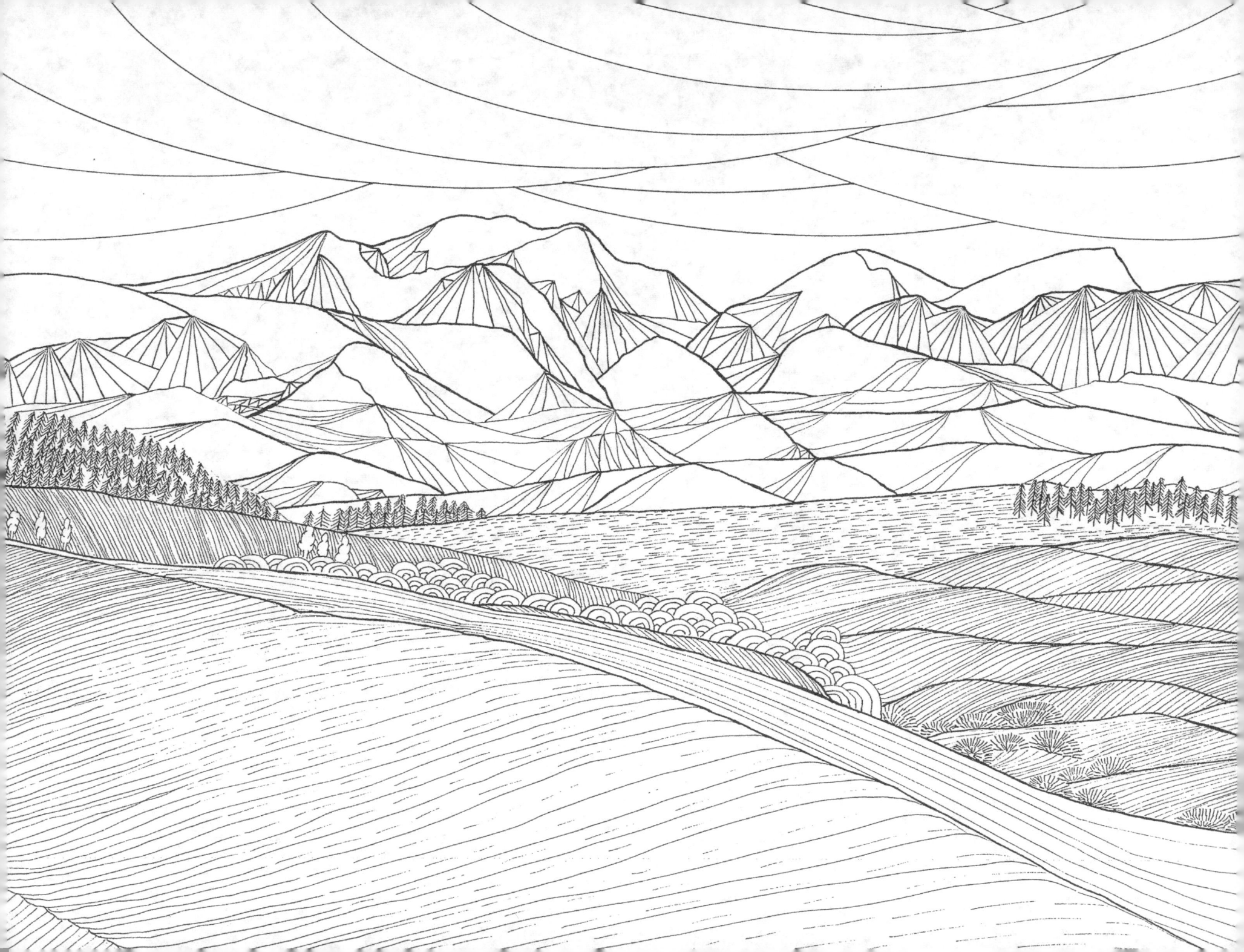

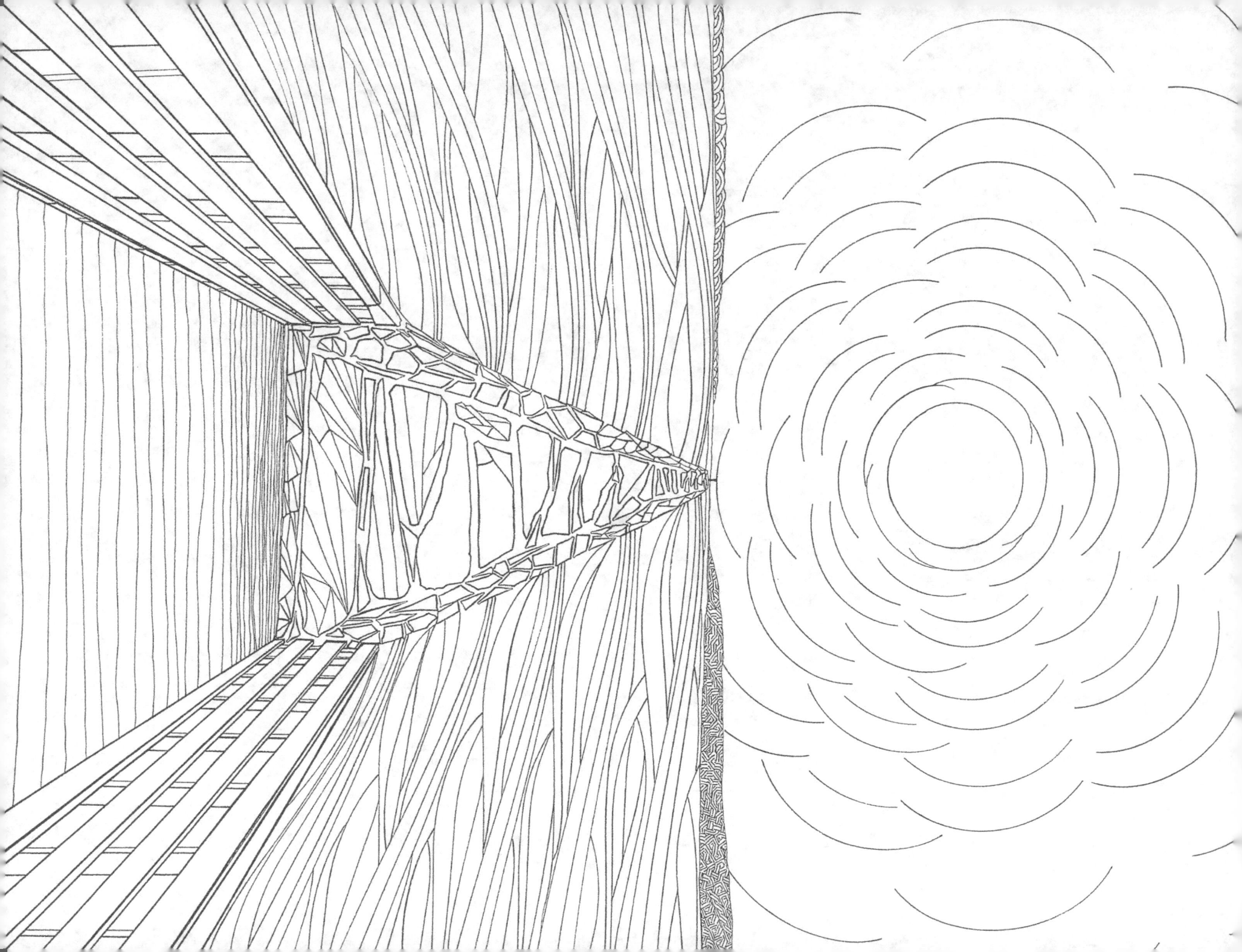

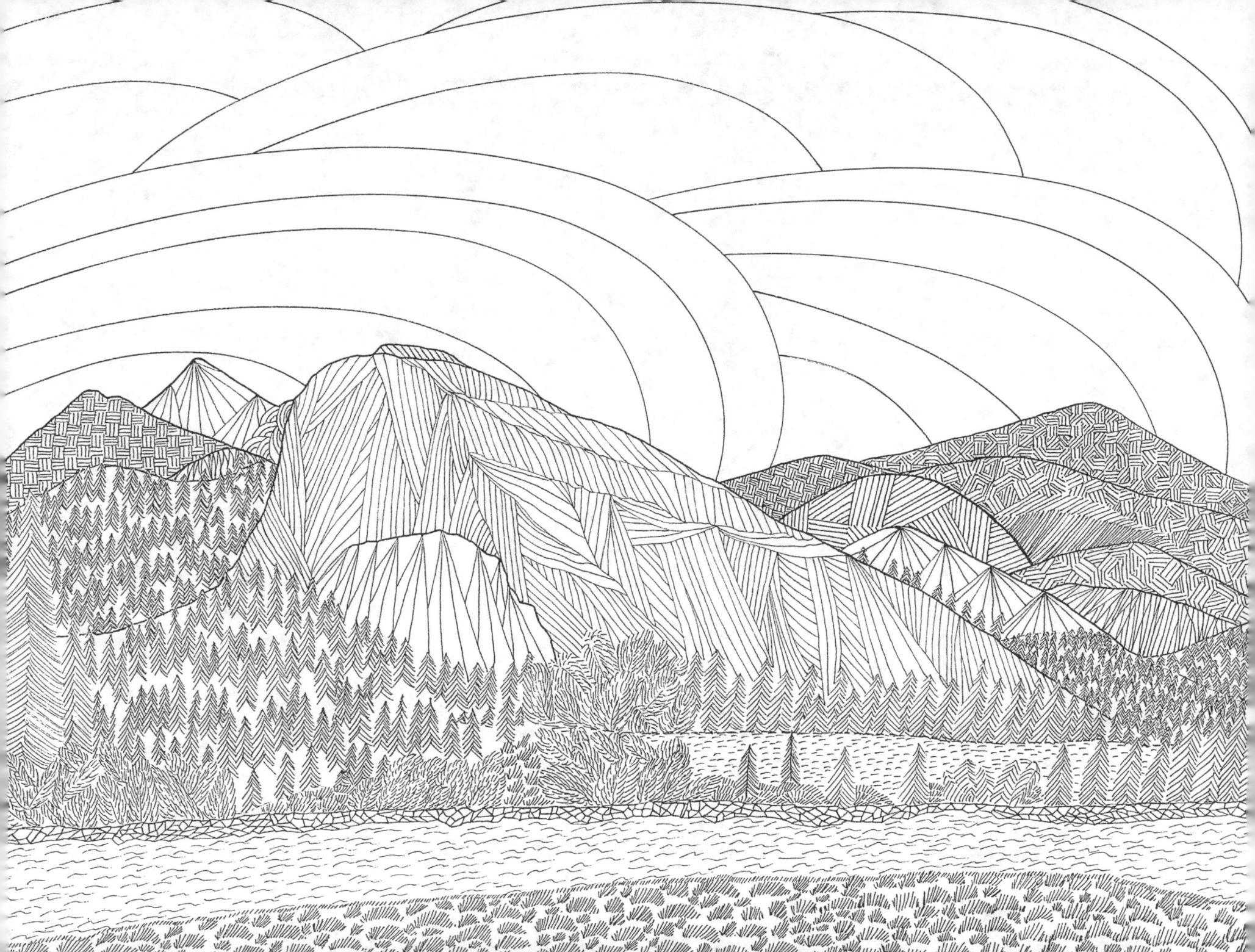

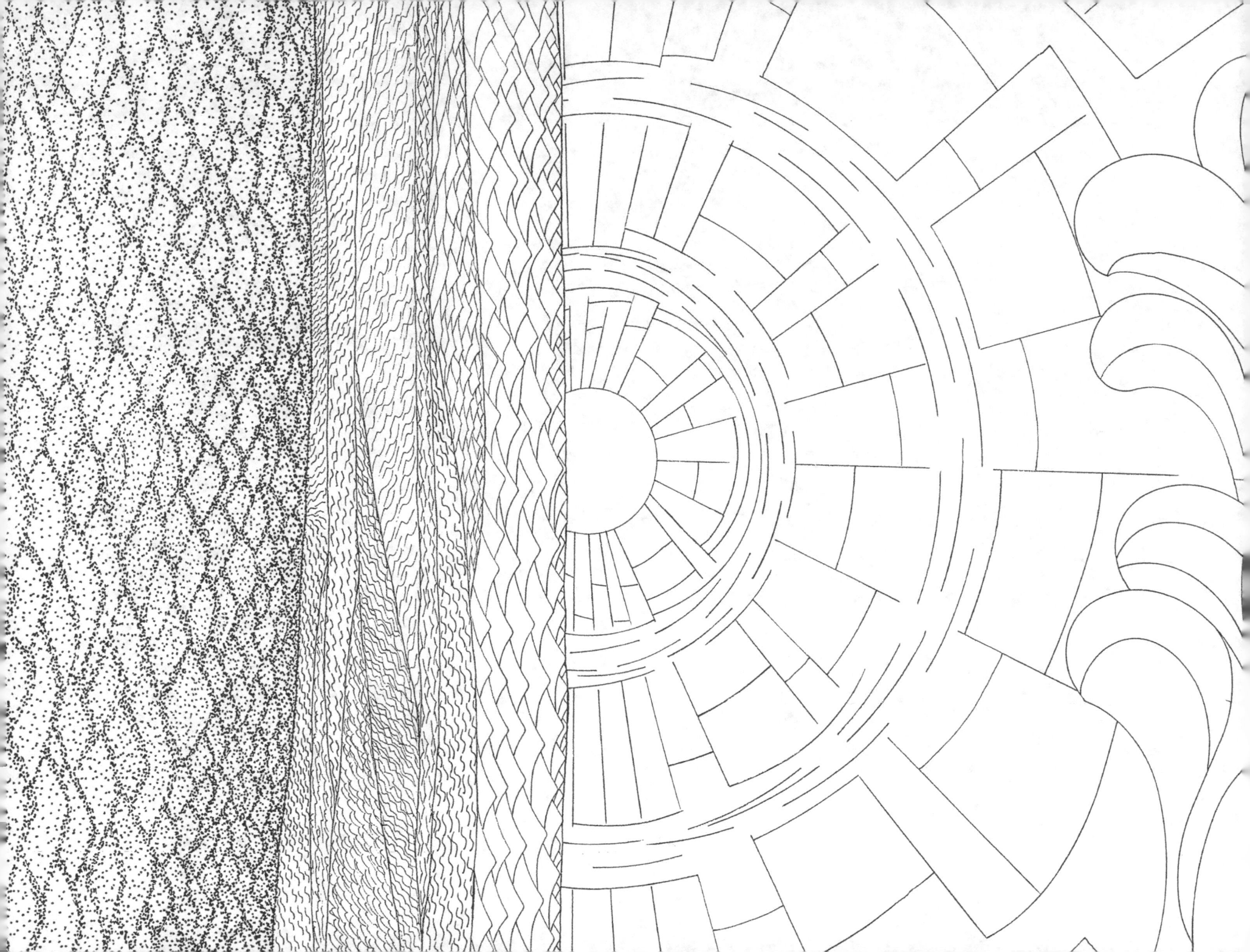

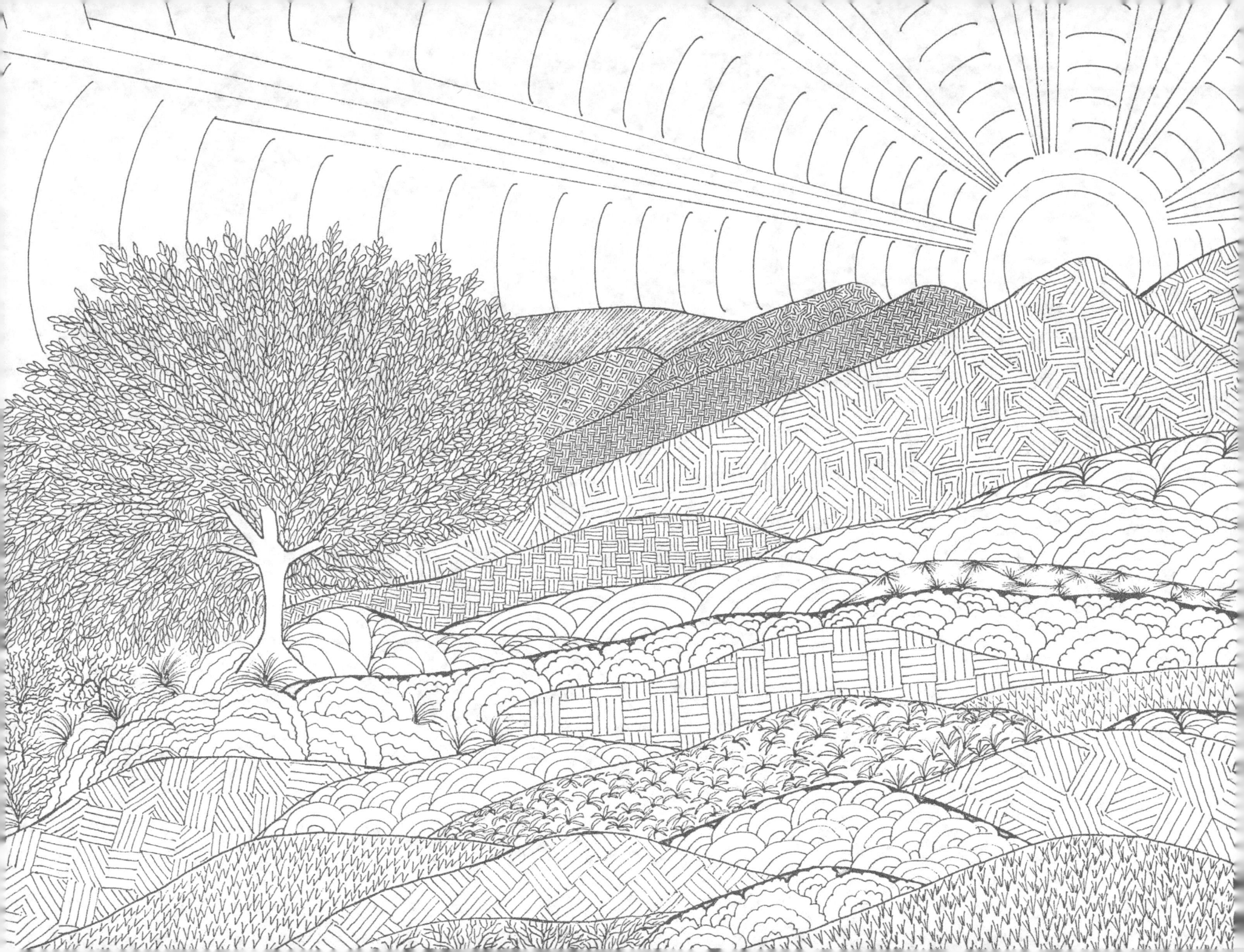

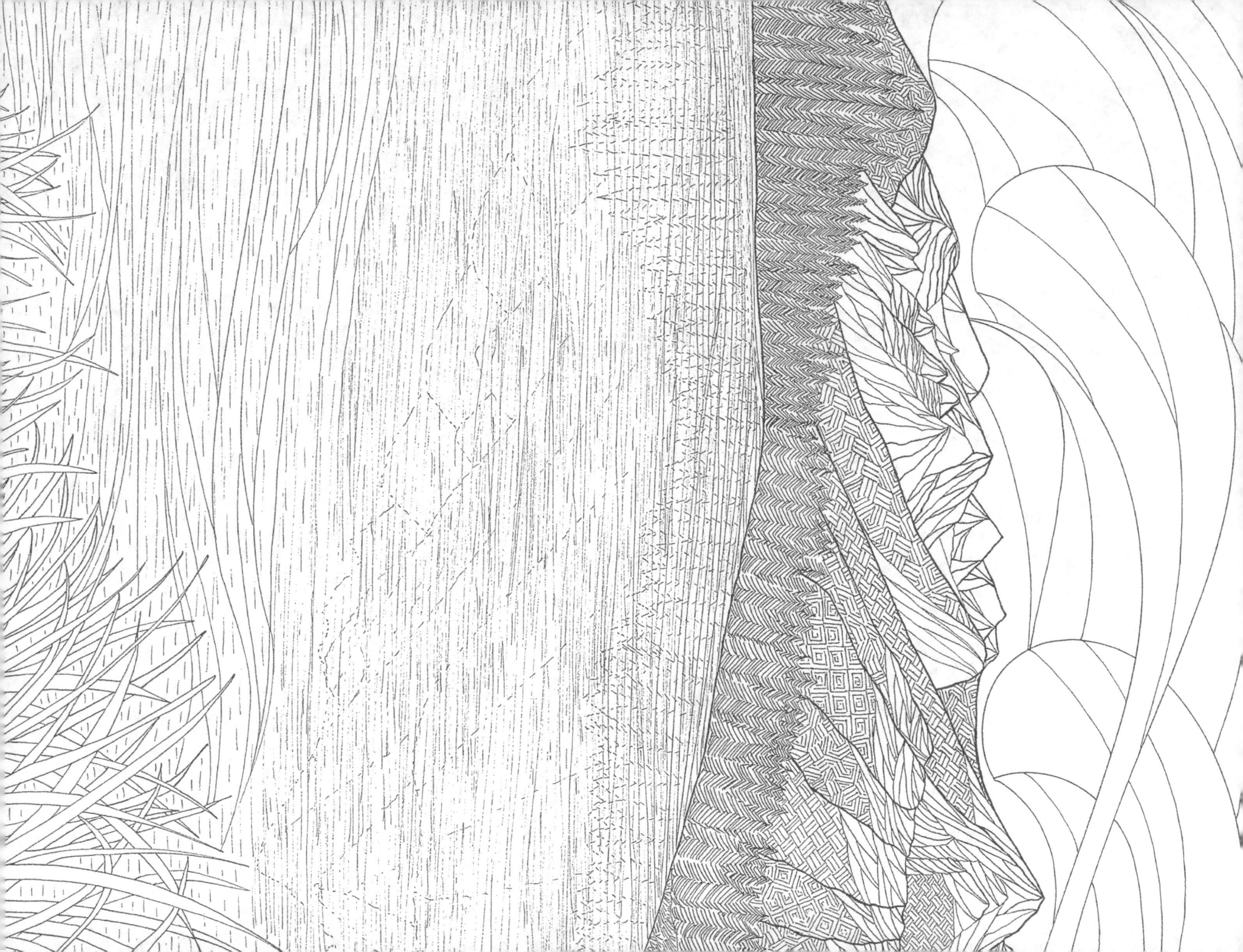

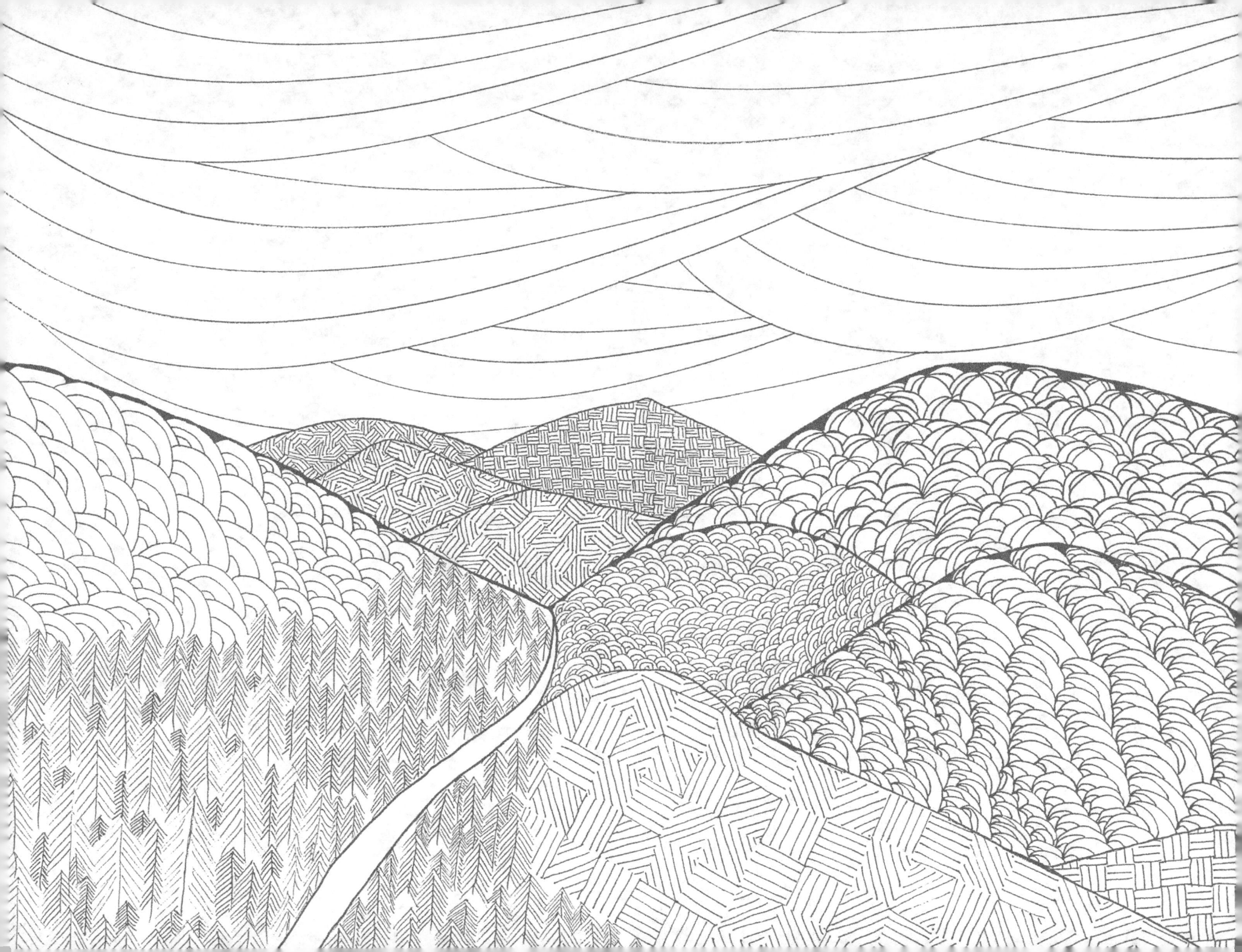

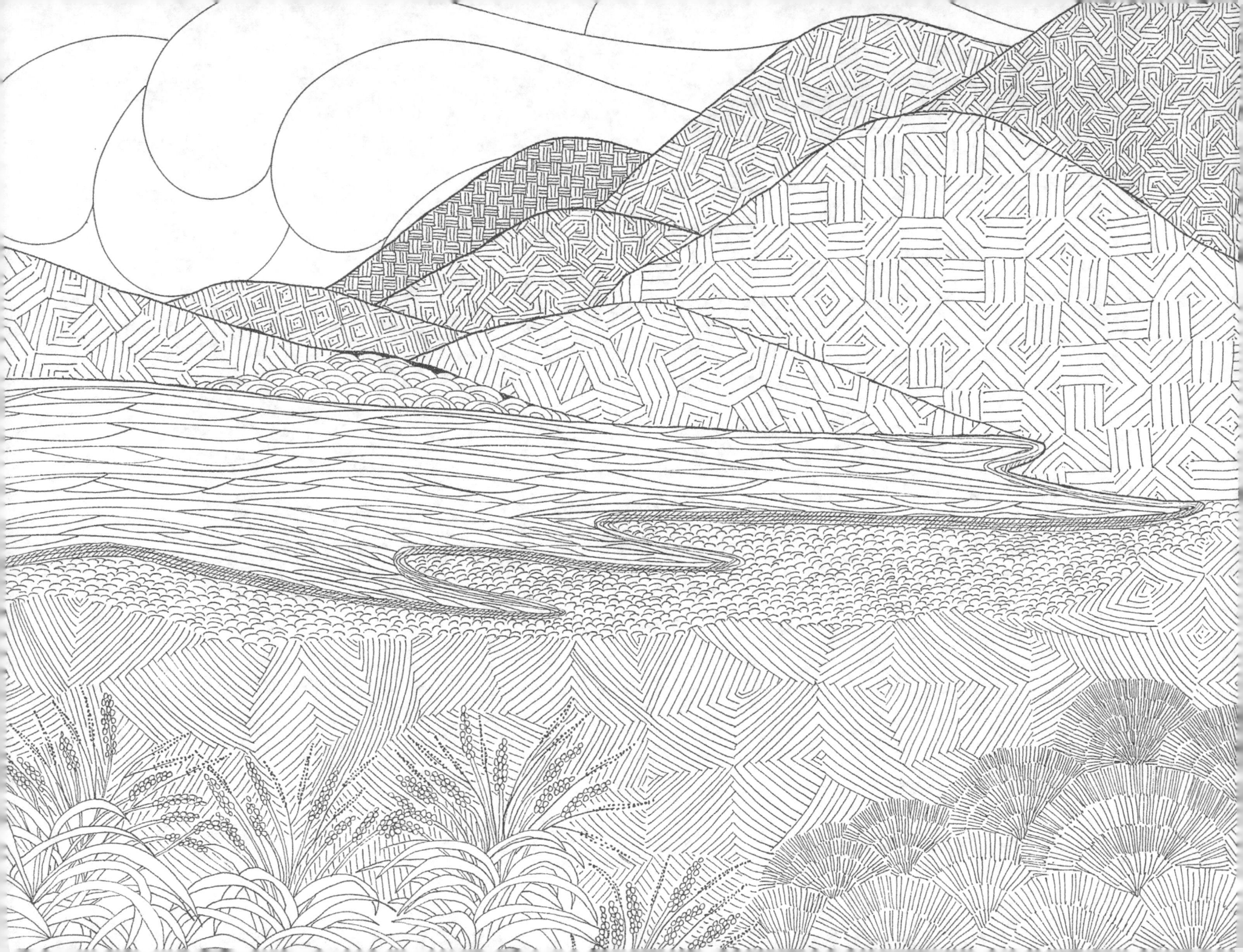

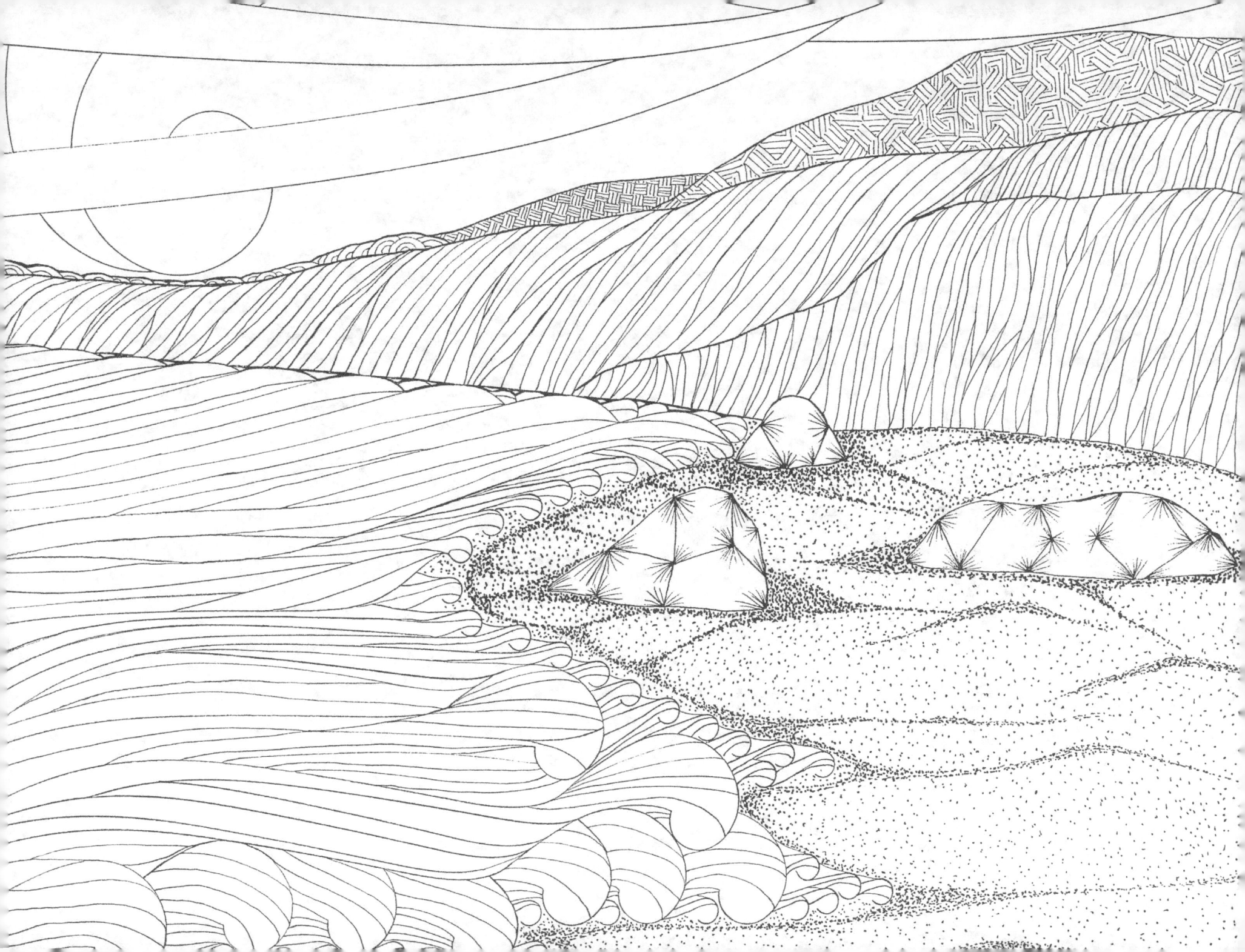

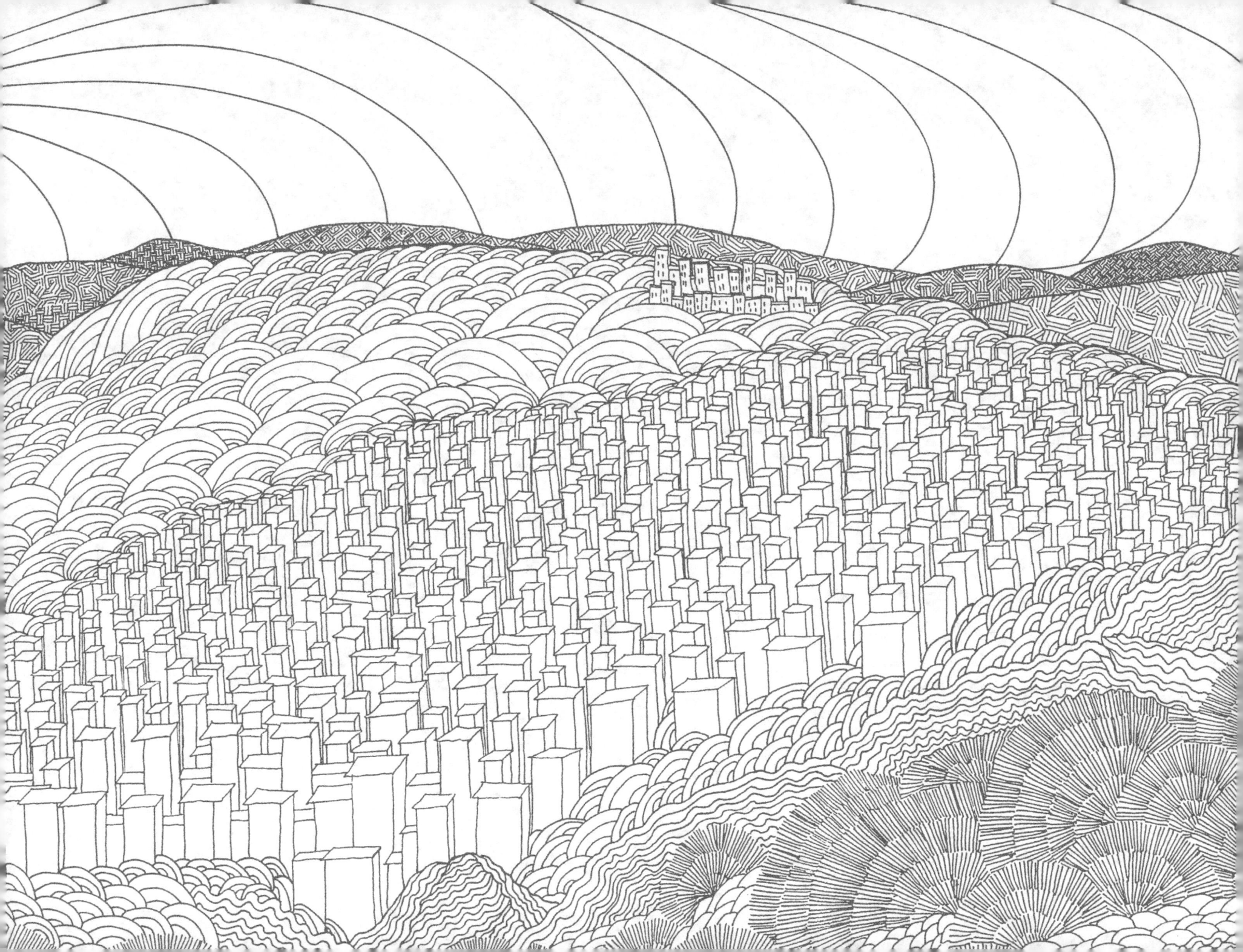

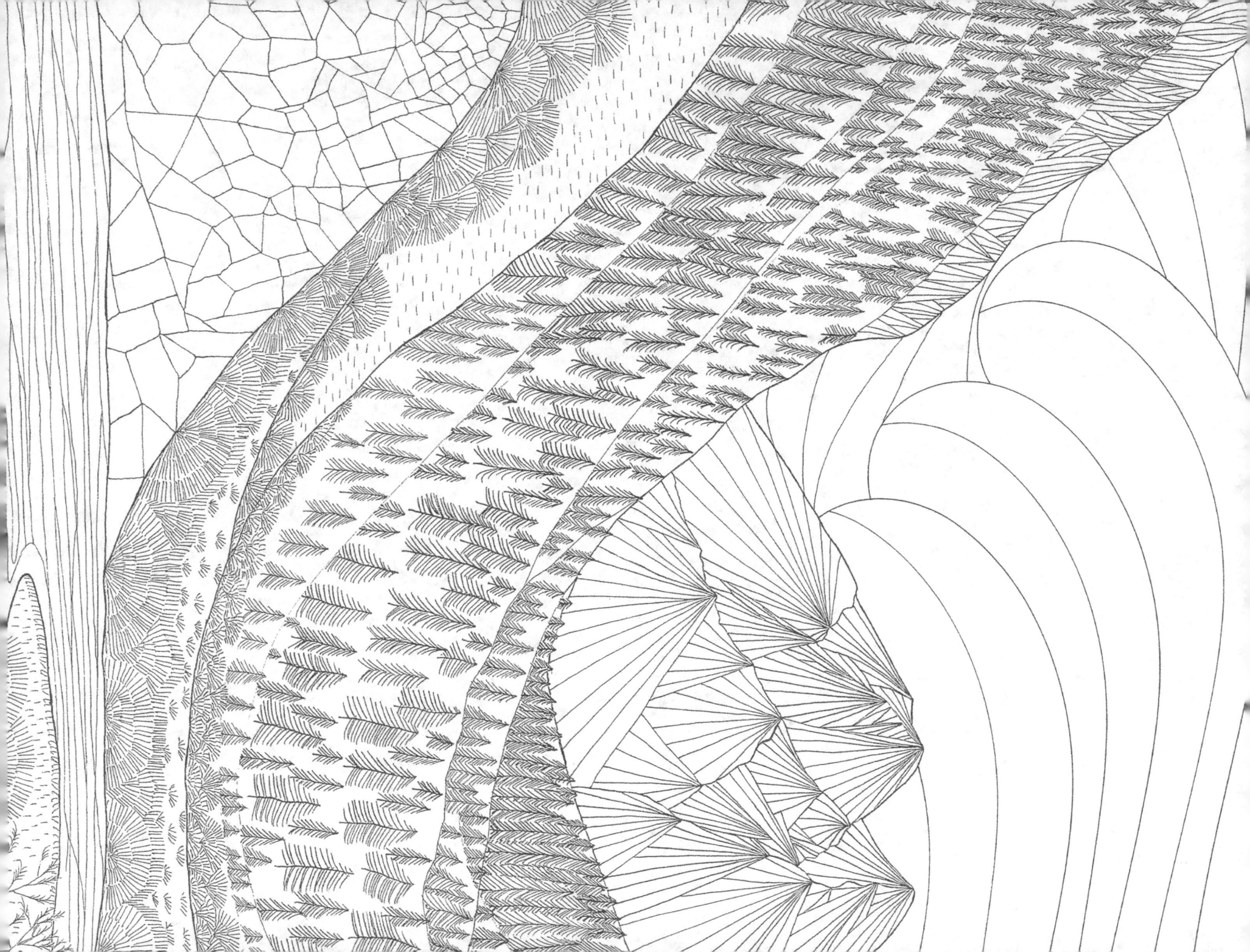

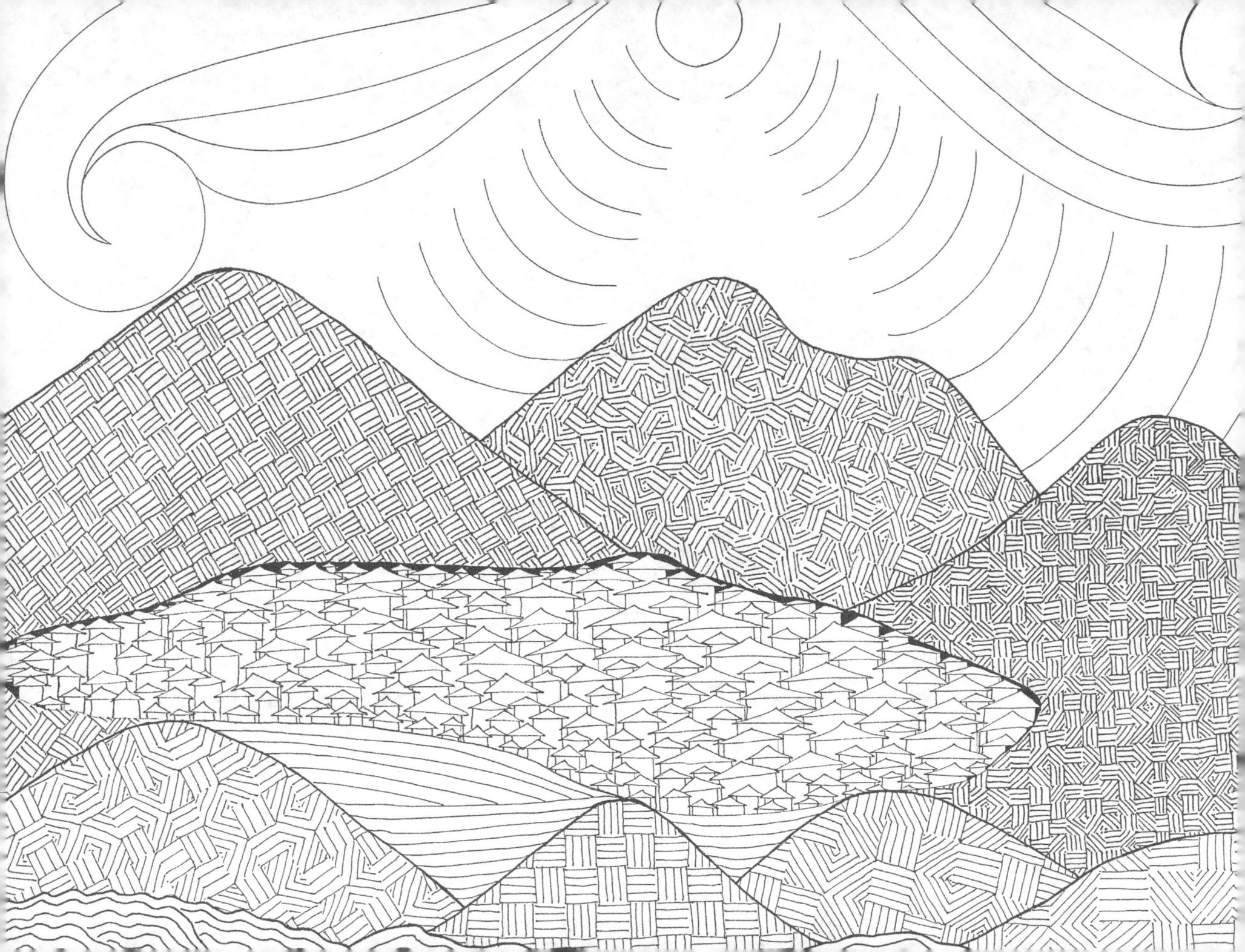

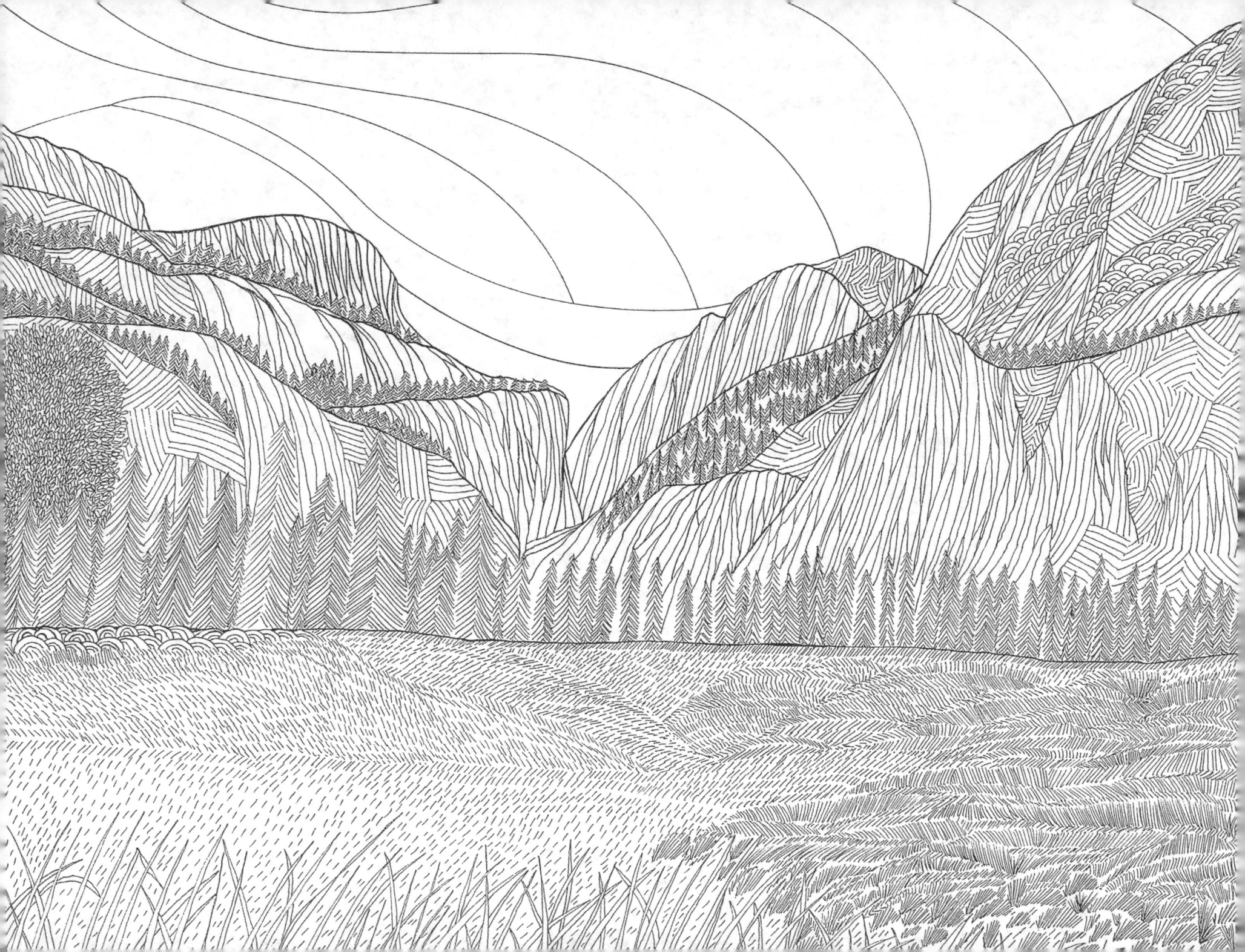

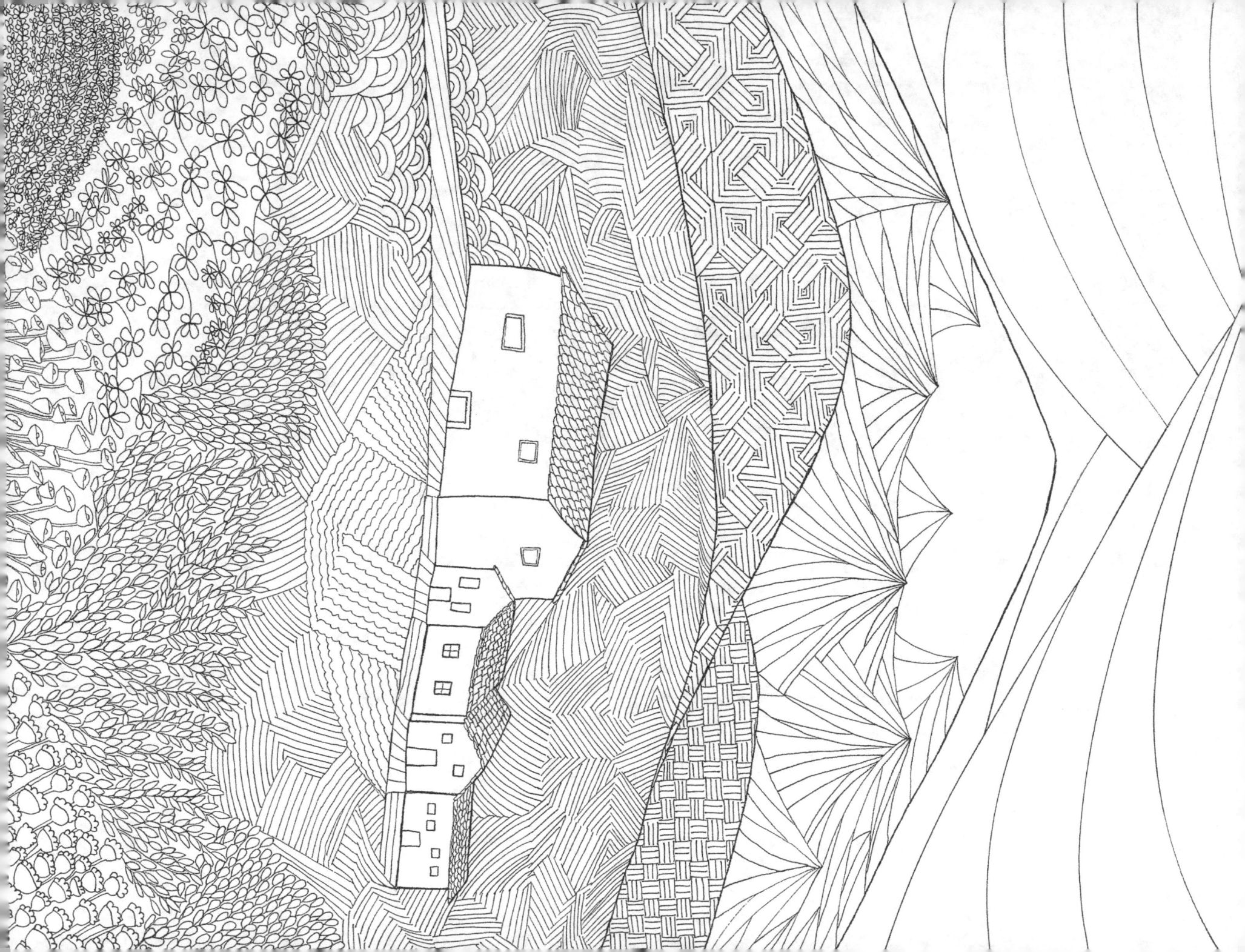

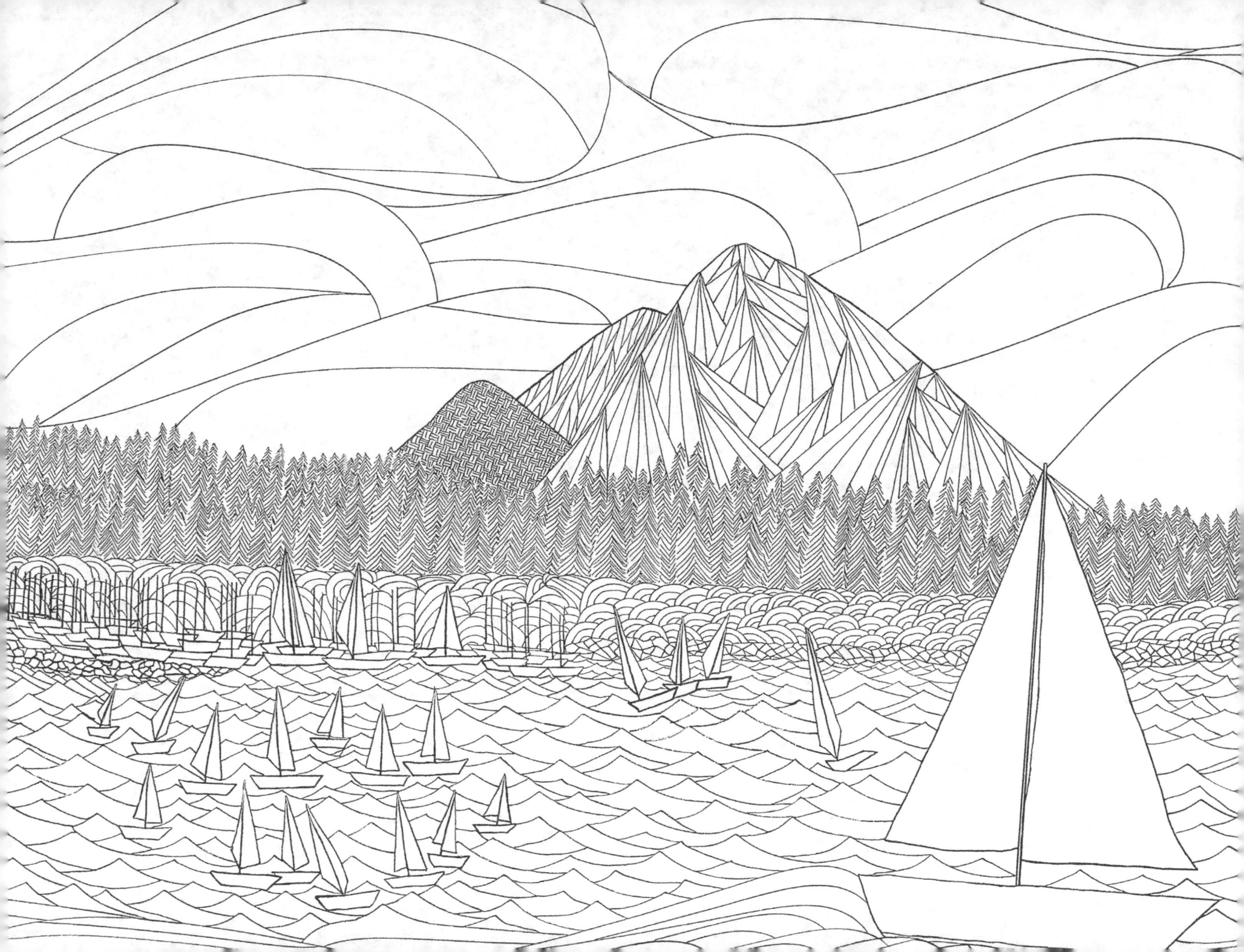

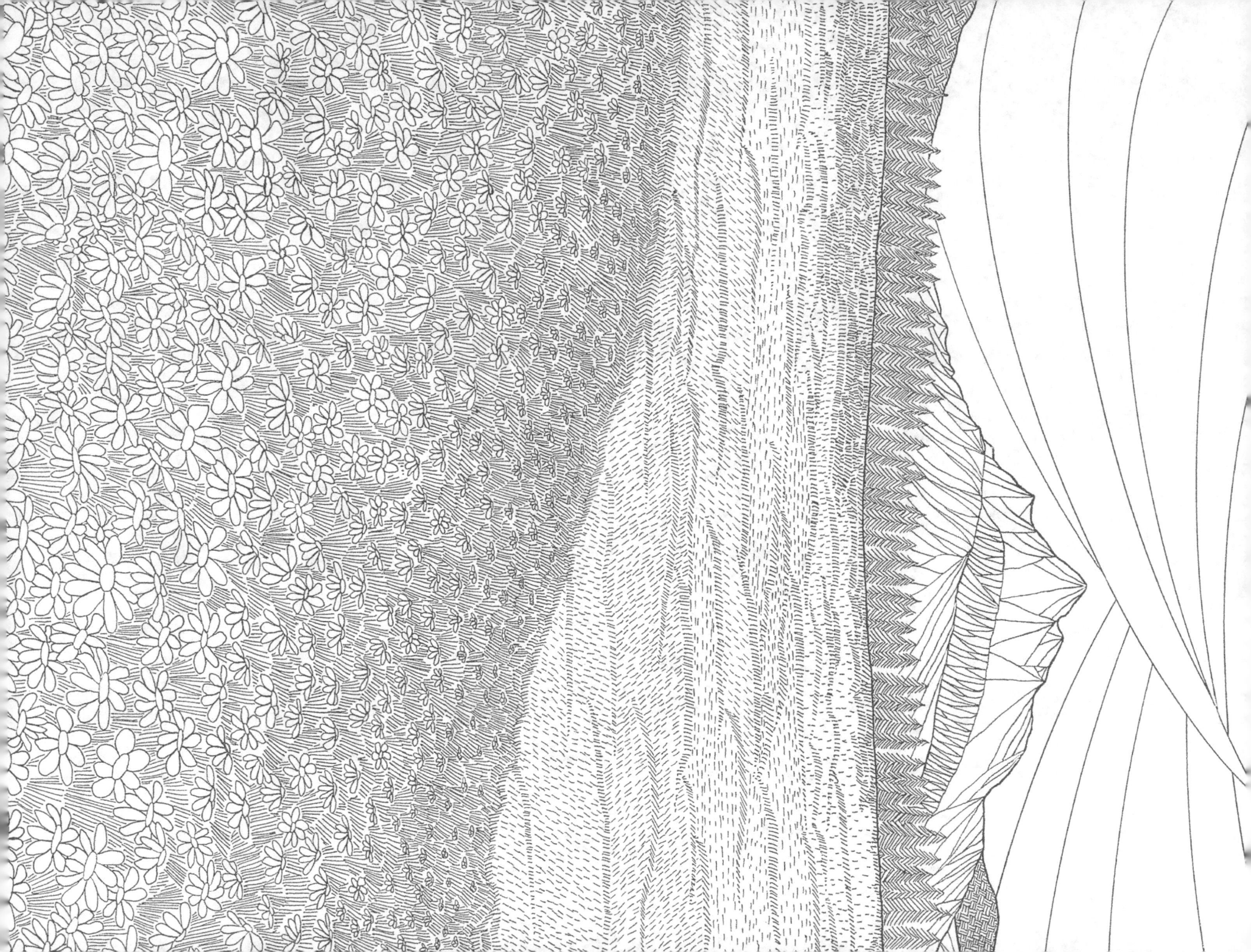

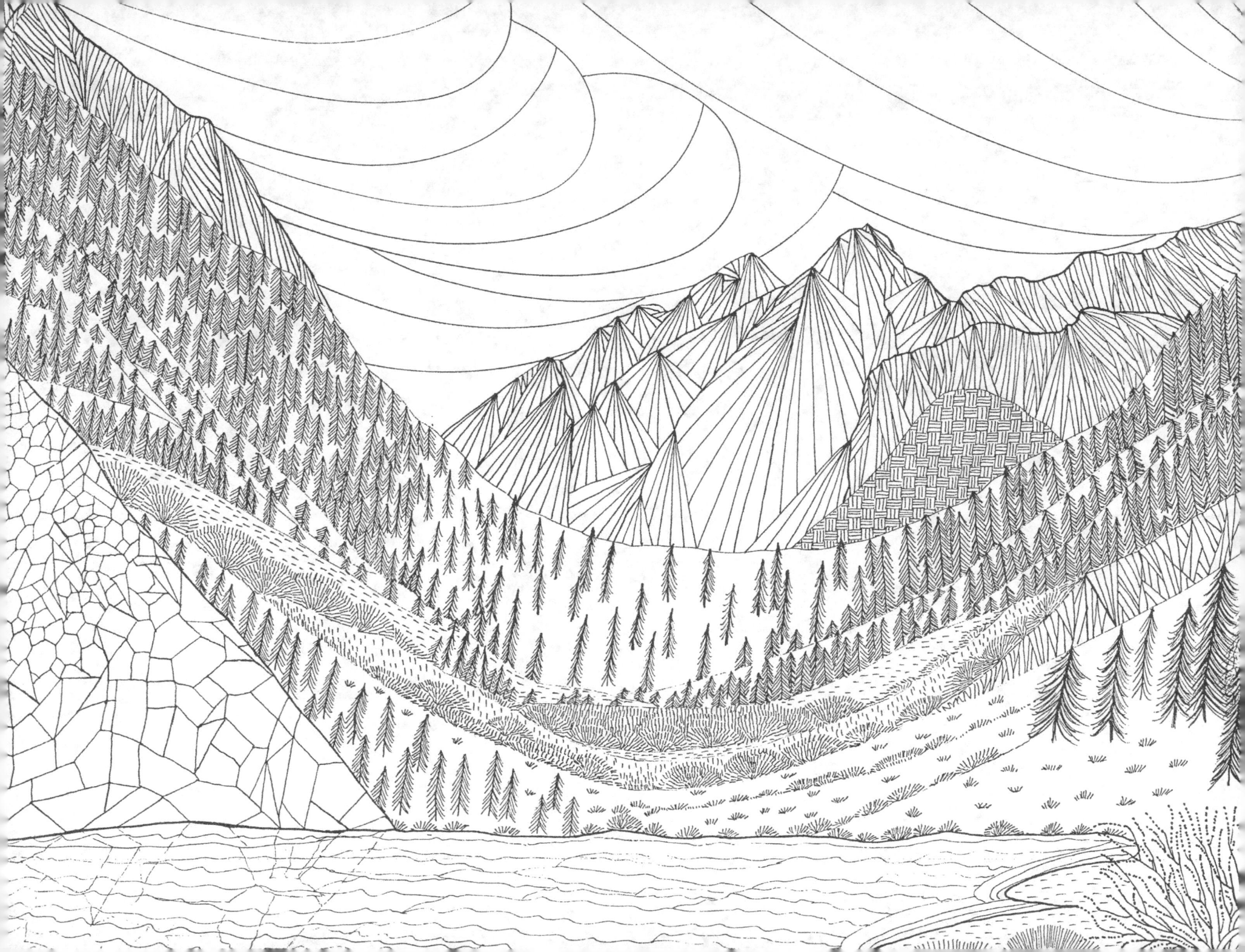

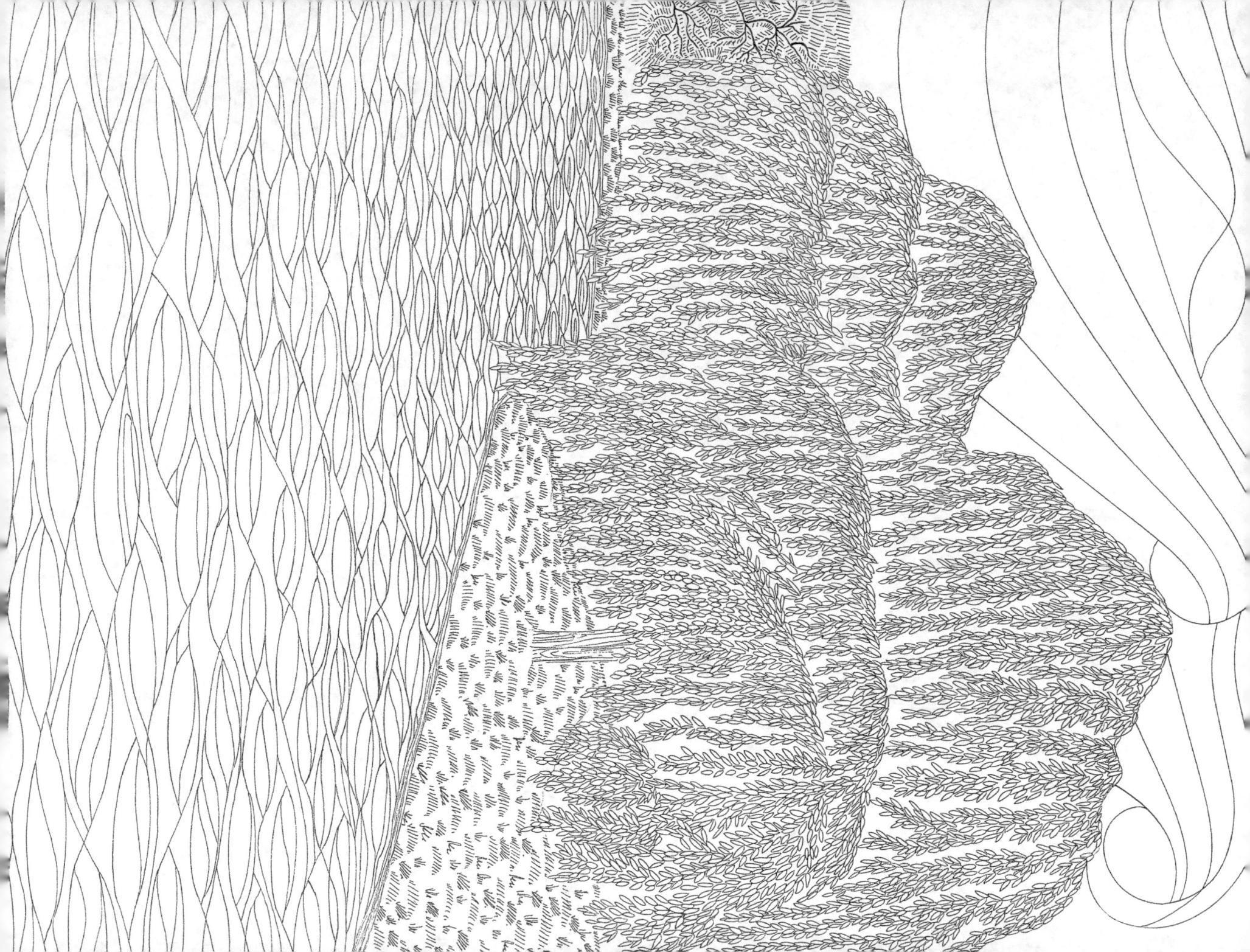

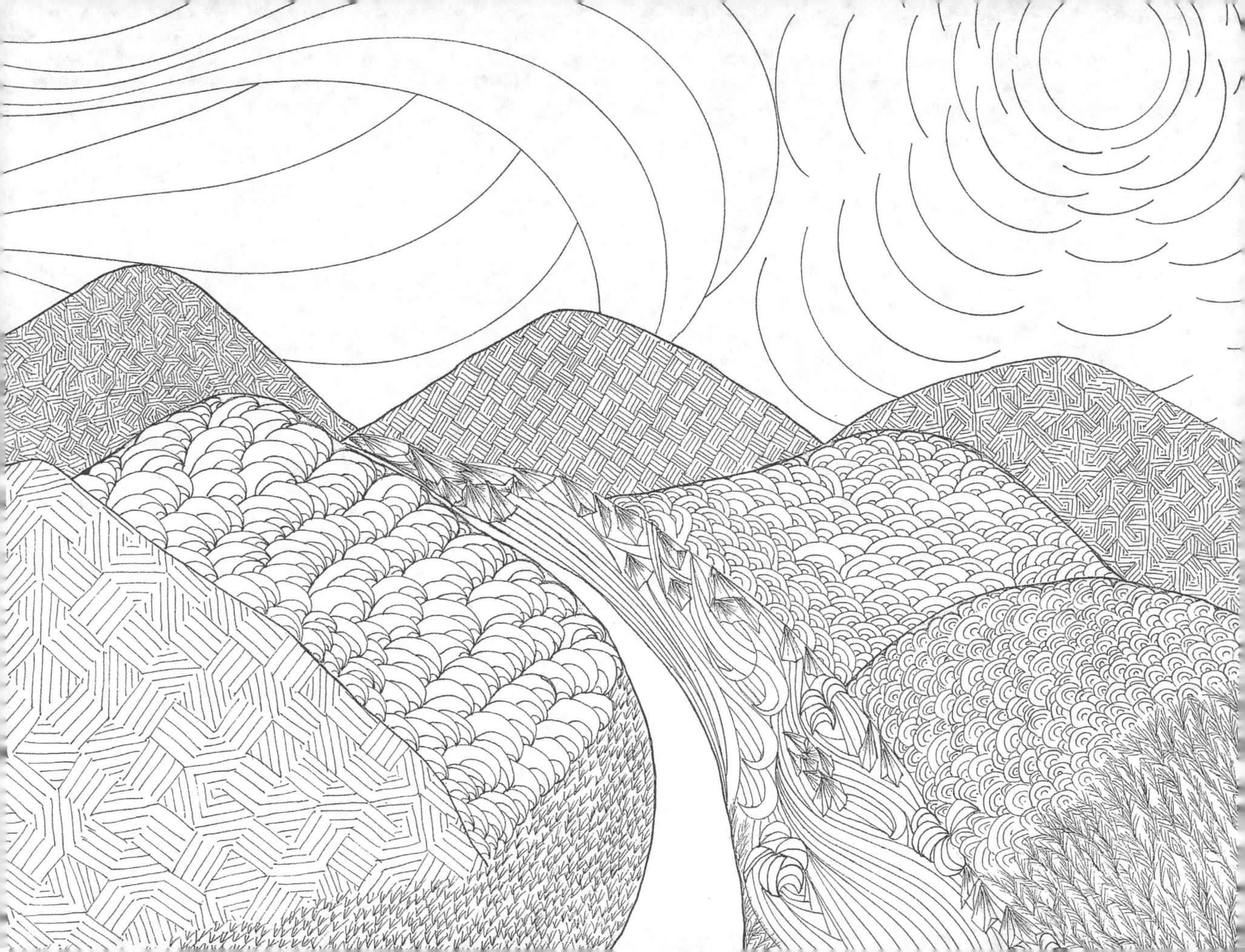

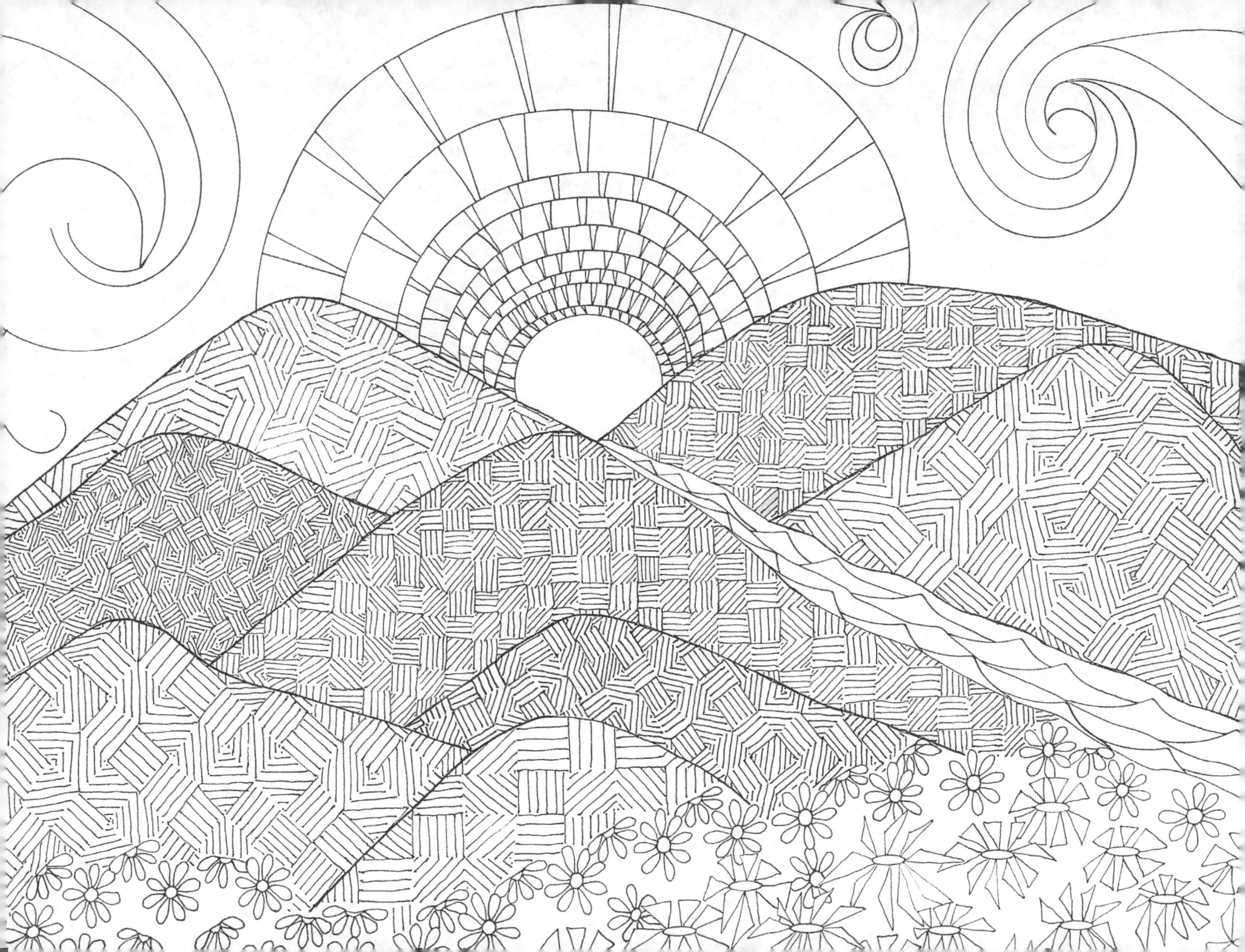

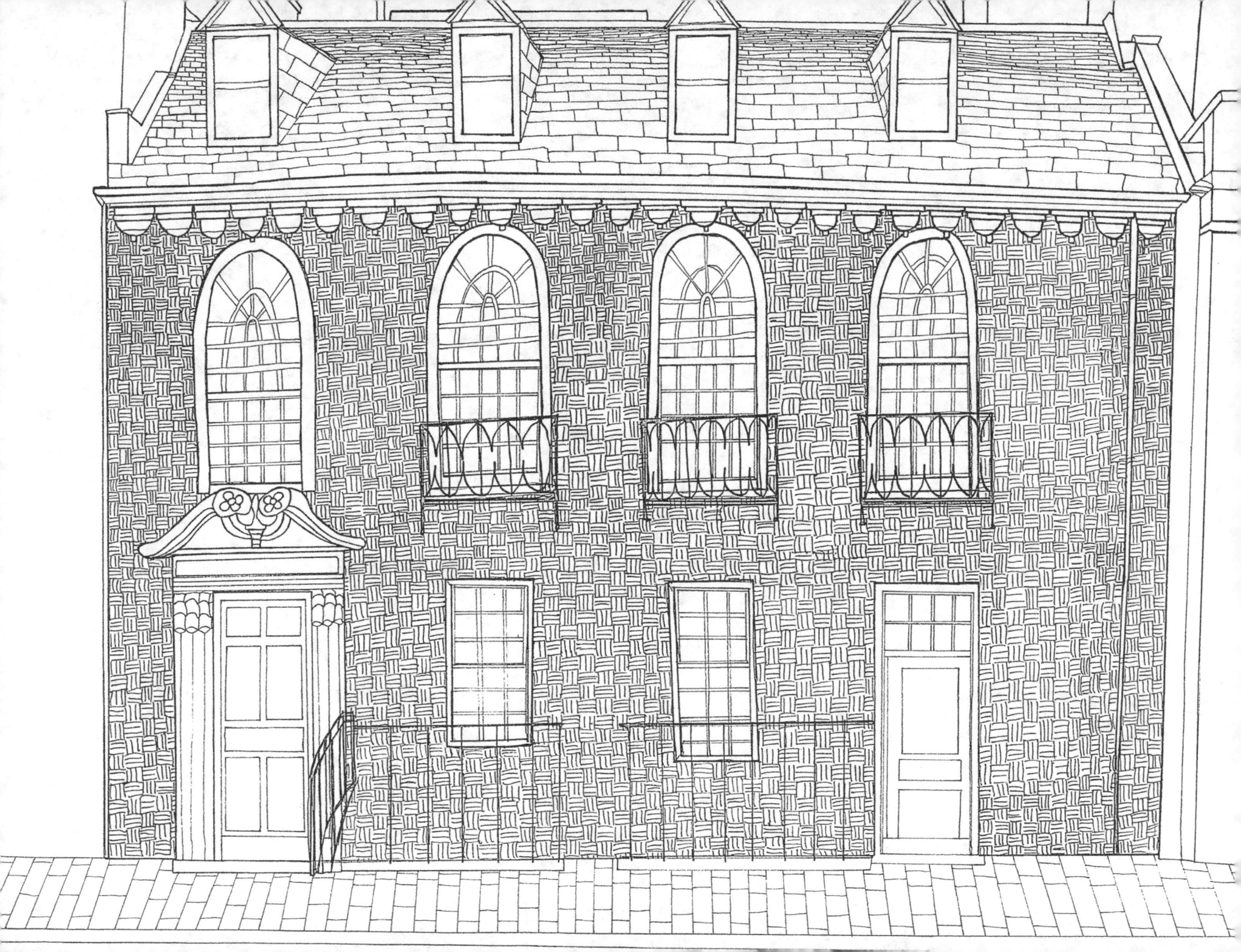

ABOUT THE ILLUSTRATOR

Mireli is an illustrator, a children's book author, and a scientist. She began drawing and painting very early. By age ten, she was creating greeting cards for family and friends. She pursued design in her early years of college, then started a family, and eventually returned to university and earned a doctorate in science. She worked in research for many years, but she always turned to art in her spare time. She is passionate about art and science, learning and creativity.

To Elise, for inspiring this book.

LINESCAPES

ISBN: 978-1523604678

The illustrations are hand drawn with digital editing.
Quotes and excerpts for poems and fairy tales are from writers in the public domain.

Elise Digga, Mirelibooks Editor

For information about sales,
please contact Miriam@MireliBooks.com

Mirelibooks.com
Cambridge, Massachusetts